PERMANENTLY
BLUE

PERMANENTLY
BLUE

How Democrats Can End the Republican
Party and Rule the Next Generation

DYLAN LOEWE

THREE RIVERS PRESS
New York

Library of Congress Cataloging-in-Publication Data

Loewe, Dylan.
    Permanently blue : how Democrats can end the
Republican party and rule the next generation /
by Dylan Loewe.—1st paperback ed.
    1. Democratic Party (U.S.)   2. Politics,
Practical—United States.   3. United States—
Politics and government—2001–2009.   I. Title.
    JK2316.L64 2009
    324.70973—dc22

                                    2010002421

ISBN 978-0-307-71799-3

Printed in the United States of America

Design by Nicola Ferguson

10   9   8   7   6   5   4   3   2   1

First Edition

For Megan

CONTENTS

Introduction

The 1790s were a pretty great time to be a member of the Federalist Party. I mean seriously great. George Washington was technically an Independent, but all of his people were Federalists. John Adams was a Federalist, as were Alexander Hamilton and Ben Franklin. All in all, some pretty heavy hitters of the day.

As political parties go, starting from scratch and electing a president on your first try is a pretty impressive feat. And it wasn't just the presidency the Federalists controlled. They had majorities in the House and the Senate and had stacked the Supreme Court with Federalist judges, including the famous Chief Justice John Marshall.

But even in the best of times, parties have a way of coming undone.

A long-brewing battle between Hamilton and President Adams boiled over in 1799 when Adams fired all of Hamilton's supporters from his cabinet. That personal rift snowballed into a party divide, paving the way for Thomas Jefferson and the Democratic-Republicans to make their move in the election of 1800. In the end, the Federalists lost the White House and Congress. They'd never get either back. A few wrong turns and the once-dominant party had spiraled into a weakened and fading minority.

That's when things really got ugly. When most people think of secession, they think of the South, of the Civil War. But nearly sixty years before the South seceded from the Union, it was the Federalists of the Northeast who were calling for dissolution. They threatened to secede over the Louisiana Purchase in 1803. A few years later, they threatened to do it again when Jefferson placed an embargo on trade with England. Federalist newspapers also started calling for secession. After thirteen years out of power, and in the midst of the War of 1812, the Federalists held a secret meeting in Hartford, Connecticut, and, according to John Quincy Adams's notes, discussed seceding from the Union and possibly joining Canada. That had to have been an odd moment for Adams, watching the party that had made his father president devolving into a secessionist fringe movement.

Awkward.

The meeting didn't stay secret long, and news of it, along with the end of the war, discredited the Federalists permanently. The collapse of the party would put the Democratic-Republicans in control of the presidency for twenty-eight years.

Fast forward to 1833. A new party, the Whigs, emerges

in opposition to Andrew Jackson and the Democratic Party. In just seven years, the party elects its first president, William Henry Harrison. To prove to the American people that he would continue to show the same strength as president that he did as war hero, Harrison gave the longest inaugural address in American history. He stood at the Capitol on a very cold and very rainy day and spoke for nearly two hours, then walked in the inaugural parade. He fell ill and died thirty-one days later.

Oops.

Harrison's vice president, John Tyler, was sworn in after Harrison's death, giving the Whigs their second president, though certainly not in the way they had hoped. The problems for the party worsened from there.

None of the party leaders had bothered to ask Tyler whether his political views were in line with the Whig agenda. Chief among the goals of the Whigs was to reestablish the Central Bank of the United States. Jackson and the Democrats had gotten rid of it. Harrison promised to bring it back during the inaugural speech that killed him. Everyone just assumed Tyler was on board.

He wasn't. When the bill reestablishing the bank arrived at his desk, he vetoed it. Just a few weeks later, he became the only sitting president to be expelled from his party.

Strike two.

The next president the Whigs elected, Zachary Taylor, also died in office, this time after just sixteen months. His replacement, Millard Fillmore, couldn't even get his own party to nominate him for reelection. By then, the party had split hard on ideological lines, with the pro- and anti-slavery wings tearing each other apart. Anti-slavery Whigs left in droves to join the Republican Party. Among them, Abraham Lincoln. Pro-slavery Whigs joined the Democrats, leaving the Whigs without a base of support from either faction. They would not reclaim national office again.

How the parties were left at that point is pretty much how they've remained. The Democrats and Republicans have been the only dominant parties in the country from the Civil War to present day. Unlike the Federalists and Whigs before them, these two parties stuck around long enough to develop the necessary organizational strength and a broad enough base of support to prevent them from ever fading entirely out of existence.

Still, that kind of institutional security does not mean there aren't serious consequences for a party that commits a number of substantial and sustained blunders.

Take the Republicans of the 1920s, for example. Warren Harding got himself elected president in 1920 by promising a "return to normalcy." As it turned out, what Harding meant by a "return to normalcy" was a return to scandal and corruption. Harding was involved in a slew of shady dealings while president. Among the friends he appointed to high-level positions, three were convicted of felonies and two committed suicide.

Harding was replaced by Calvin Coolidge, who governed as an absentee president and who helped put the

American economy on track toward the Great Depression. His replacement, Herbert Hoover, was there for the crash, and his inability to stop the bleeding was enough to send the Republican Party into a tailspin. The party didn't cease to exist after the 1932 election, but for twenty years, they lost the White House. And for fifty-six of the next sixty-two years, they lost control of the House of Representatives.

It isn't all that rare for parties to stumble through history, to see their success ebb and flow over time. But there are moments—once, maybe twice in a century—when a political party can operate so dysfunctionally that it can find itself marginalized into long-term minority status— into spending an entire generation out of power.

For today's Republican Party, this is one of those moments.

ONE

☆ ☆ ☆

The Possibility

The Democrats haven't been this happy since 2000 when **CNN** *declared for Al Gore. And that lasted all of about an hour.*

—*Rahm Emanuel*

In the summer of 2006, two months before the Democrats would take back the House of Representatives, freshman Senator Barack Obama took a trip to his father's continent. He began in South Africa, where he toured the prison that housed Nelson Mandela during his twenty-seven-year incarceration. He visited Ethiopia and Chad and saw both slum and savannah. Finally, Obama arrived in Kenya. He visited his grandmother, who he communicates with only through a translator, and then he and his wife Michelle took HIV tests publicly, urging the thousands who had gathered to watch to do the same. Toward the end of the trip, they traveled to one of the worst slums anywhere on the planet.

Almost a third of Nairobi's population is jammed into Kibera, a single square mile with no running water, where thousands are orphaned and most are squatters. It is one of the saddest, most wretched places imaginable, full of death, disease, and hopelessness. As the Obamas approached the town, a group of young boys at the outskirts saw them, and with excitement turned skipping and shouting toward the center of the slum:

"Obama biro, yawne yo! Obama biro yawne, yo!"

"Obama's coming. Clear the way."

Twenty-six months later, on a Grant Park stage overlooking the Chicago skyline, Barack Obama claimed the American presidency. He had confounded expectations, besting John McCain after defeating the most powerful political machine within his own party. He ran on a message of hope and a dramatic call for change; with the support of millions of donors, volunteers, and believers, and on a wave of the $750 million his movement raised, Obama emerged on that Chicago stage as history personified.

The win was undeniably earth-shattering. In terms of political strategy, it was a masterpiece. But its most consequential legacy was not settled that night. The events that were set in motion years before, and those that powered his victory, have positioned the Democratic Party to be the dominant force in American politics, not just for four or eight years, or even a decade. After November 2008, for the first time in its history, the Democratic Party is poised to secure a permanent majority.

What do I mean by permanent majority? I'm not talking about Democrats taking control of the U.S. government for as long as there continue to be united states. But I do mean something substantial. Democrats have the opportunity to maintain control of Congress and the White House for an entire generation—for the next twenty-four years. That's three consecutive two-term presidencies and twelve congressional elections.

It's never been done before. Not once. But that isn't to say the Democrats haven't come close at least a couple of times.

In 1932, during the Depression that both started and worsened under Republican rule, Franklin Roosevelt emerged to obliterate the Republican Party in that year's presidential election. Roosevelt won forty-two states, and with them, swept Democrats into power on a virtual tidal wave. The party picked up ninety-seven seats in the House and thirteen in the Senate. And they just kept winning after that. Republicans continued to campaign against FDR's popular New Deal, striking a tone eerily familiar to the GOP of 2010. They railed against socialist takeovers and out-of-control spending. They decried attempts to expand the role of government, whatever the cause. In 1936, Alf Landon, the Republican nominee, declared, "I do not believe that a temporary depression is adequate reason for changing our whole form of government!"

FDR responded with characteristic ridicule, dismissing the Republicans while egging them on. Just days before the election, at Madison Square Garden in New York City, Roosevelt proclaimed, "Never before in all of our history have these forces been so united against one candidate as they stand today." He paused. "They are unanimous in their hatred for me and I welcome their hatred!"

The audience roared with applause and erupted at the rallying cry, and, come election day, so did the Democratic Party. They had done so well that they earned a 334 to 88 majority in the House. When, two years later, they suffered a loss of seventy-two seats, the majority they were left with was still substantially larger than the one Democrats enjoy today (they lost seven seats in the Senate and still had sixty-nine to spare). Democrats continued to control both chambers until 1946.

By then, World War II had been won, Roosevelt had died, and one of the most unpopular presidents in American history had been sworn in to replace him. Though remembered fondly by history, Harry Truman's approval rating dropped to 32 percent by the time the 1946 midterms came around. He was seen as ineffective on a number of issues and was plagued by the Republican mantra, "To err is Truman."

During his time in office, the Democrats lost and regained control of the House and Senate a couple of times, fighting the same narrow battle year after year. But by 1954, the Democrats had regained their dominance as Congress's majority party. After the '54 midterms, the Democrats would hold the Senate and House continuously for twenty-six years. They lost the Senate in 1980, but didn't lose the House until 1994, a full forty years after taking control of the chamber. They were so dominant that in the sixty-eight years between FDR's first election and the end of the twentieth century, Republicans controlled the House for only ten total years and the Senate for only sixteen.

The Democratic majorities were no doubt deep and long lasting, but their effectiveness in pushing a progressive agenda was often muted, if not entirely obstructed, by the presence of a Republican in the White House. Without a Democratic president, the congressional majority became more about preventing the White House from enacting its agenda than it did about making meaningful progress on its own. In 2007 and 2008, for example, Democratic control of Congress helped prevent George W. Bush's administration from further enacting its right-wing agenda, but Democrats failed to bring forth much meaningful legislation. Non-binding resolutions against the Iraq war were passed. A few bills were sent to the president's desk for veto. But for the most part, the Democrats' efforts during the Bush administration were more akin to prevent-defense than an offensive drive down the field.

Contrast that with Congress in 1965 and 1966. Barry Goldwater's disastrous presidential campaign in 1964 had utterly ravaged the hopes of down ballot Republicans. On his blog, David Frum, a speechwriter to the second President Bush, described the 1964 race as "an unredeemed and unmitigated catastrophe for Republicans and conservatives." The Democrats picked up thirty-six seats in the

House and two in the Senate, swelling their majorities in both chambers to more than two-thirds.

Heading into his first full term, Lyndon Johnson had overwhelming majorities in both chambers; Democrats used that power to make some of the biggest strides forward in the progressive agenda since the New Deal. They passed the Voting Rights Act. They passed Medicare and Medicaid. They expanded anti-poverty programs and passed the Higher Education Act and the Freedom of Information Act. They passed major air pollution legislation, increased safety standards for cars, and did away with national-origin quotas on immigration, all in those years.

That's what sizable majorities can get you, but only when the White House and Congress are controlled by the same party. Traditionally, that's been the tricky part. Since FDR's presidency, only once has a party held the White House for longer than eight years. In fact, the same party controlled both the White House and Congress for just twenty of the last fifty years. It occurred for more than four consecutive years just once.

When George W. Bush won the White House, for example, it was the first time that Republicans controlled Congress and the White House since the first two years of Eisenhower's administration. Bill Clinton spent only two of his eight years with a Democratic Congress. Nixon, Ford, Reagan, and H. W. Bush—none of them ever had the opportunity.

Dominating Congress is important; the power of that branch to influence policy should not be understated.

But controlling Congress alone isn't enough. To have a true majority—to have actual control over the political agenda—a party has to control the White House, as well.

That's the kind of permanent majority the Democrats are on the verge of building: a single party, democratically elected to control the Senate, the House of Representatives, and the White House without interruption for an entire generation. It's never happened before; until 2008, the opportunity never existed. But on the heels of Obama's victory, the Democrats are as close as they've ever come to having that chance. The possibility is very real.

I know what you must be thinking, and I agree: A concept that bold deserves to be accompanied by a healthy dose of skepticism. It's never once been done before. And it's asking a lot from a party that hasn't always been up to the task. But that it hasn't happened yet, in truth, holds very little bearing on whether it will this time. The past isn't always the best measure of the future—especially with the kind of dramatic changes we see in the way political campaigns unfold.

In 2008, for example, Obama raised over $500 million on the Internet. Four years earlier, Howard Dean shocked the world when he raised just $27 million the same way. Four years before that—no online campaign to speak of. Back up another eight—no Internet.

How politics operates presently is so dramatically more sophisticated than it was when Bill Clinton first ran for president that the systems are barely comparable. And it's not just the Internet. Before 2002, soft money was the name of the political game—donors could give unlimited donations to political parties to be spent on behalf of candidates. The Bipartisan Campaign Finance Reform Act, commonly known as McCain-Feingold, changed all that, and in doing so, unintentionally introduced a new beast onto the political stage: the 527. In 2004, John Kerry's campaign was left unprepared for attacks from 527 organizations like the Swift Boat Veterans for Truth in part because no such group had yet come into existence.

History becomes an even murkier indicator of potential future changes when we start talking in generation-long periods. The first presidential debate wasn't held until 1960. We didn't even have a Federal Election Commission until 1975, and we didn't start using the modern primary system until 1976. We didn't have Super Tuesday until 1988. MSNBC and Fox News weren't launched until 1996. A skepticism rooted in history is reasonable, but in this case, it results in a faulty analogy. It's a different game today, barely recognizable when compared to the campaigns of less than a decade ago.

Enter Barack Obama, his election itself an unlikely historical event, and the twenty-first-century Democratic Party. Just a few years ago, most Democratic campaigns could be described as sloppy and blunder-prone, with the party unable to articulate a clear message or produce a decent national candidate. But Democrats made enormous strides in the 2008 election. They now enjoy long-term organizational and political advantages that are more one-sided than at any time since the Great Depression.

That the Republican Party is collapsing in on itself certainly doesn't hurt. But Democrats need not rely solely on GOP self-destruction to deliver their majority. Along the way, they built an unprecedented—perhaps unmatchable—political apparatus that will help them maintain control of the White House and help them defend their congressional majorities.

At the same time, demographic changes and political realignments are conspiring to provide the Democratic Party with an atmosphere ripe for sustaining a majority for a quarter century. During the last ten years, minorities have accounted for 80 percent of the population growth in the United States. And in the 2008 presidential election, 80 percent of minorities voted for Barack Obama. That increase accounted for Obama's victories in New Mexico, Colorado, Florida, and Nevada (among others), and will help ensure the durability of the Democratic Party. Where populations are growing, the country is also liberalizing. The fastest-growing suburbs of Virginia, North Carolina, and Pennsylvania helped deliver those states to Obama. As that growth continues, so too will Democratic dominance.

Today's Democratic Party has arrived at a confluence of events: a once-in-a-generation politician; a newly built, unmatchable political apparatus, the most sophisticated in history; an upcoming redistricting; a country that is getting younger, more ethnic, more liberal; and a Republican Party that's self-destructing. It's an extraordinary opportunity; if the Democrats don't squander it, the twenty-first-century Democratic Party will control American politics continuously through 2032, perhaps beyond.

This book is like a journey through time, but without a DeLorean. We'll start in 2009 with Obama's inauguration and the devolution of the Republican Party. We'll take a look at the 2010 midterms, move through to Obama's reelection and the eventual search for his successor, and examine how changes in our political landscape will, over time, reshape American politics for a generation.

On that journey, there are just a few ground rules, all of which are worth considering, even if you can't help but ignore them.

RULE #1: TAKE THE LONG VIEW.

The Democrats are about to lose a ton of seats in the 2010 midterm elections. They'll still retain their majorities in the House and Senate, but it's hard to envision a scenario where they don't come out of November pretty badly bruised. If you were to look at the chances of Democrats building a long-term durable majority based solely on the events unfolding right now, it would be hard to argue that things are going to go well anytime soon.

But we are about to embark on a twenty-four-year-long journey. Along the way there will be bad moments for Democrats; there's no question about that. But they will be just that: moments. Moments on a much broader time-line. The Republicans can keep shoveling the snow off the walkway, but they can't stop the impending avalanche.

What happens in the 2010 midterms is the least relevant data point for determining what will happen for the Democrats long term. As you'll read in this book, in the years that follow the midterms, there will be seismic changes in everything, from the shapes of the districts congresspeople compete in to the makeup of the voters who will elect them.

In order to look through it, you have to see past the current moment, take the longer view, see the broader context. And that starts by not letting the news cycle carry you away. The difficulty of that is understandable. New media, old media, it's all to blame. The twenty-four-hour news cycle, the minute-to-minute blogosphere, the constant chatter of social networks—all of it tends to give the impression that any single day, any given moment, is especially important.

If the president chooses his words carelessly, within minutes Twitter will be abuzz. A few minutes after that, the blogosphere begins to chatter. An hour later, cable news has the video and begins covering the moment, replaying the clip a few times every hour. The focus shifts, and with it, the news cycle. For a day, perhaps more, a slipup or a negative story or a small setback is amplified, linked to, and tweeted about. Relinked. Re-tweeted.

As it reverberates through that echo chamber, it's hard not to assign it a broader meaning. But just because it got a lot of attention doesn't mean it matters at all in the long run. And just because media outlets choose to speculate wildly doesn't mean that they have any idea what they're talking about.

The media feeds on itself; it requires a constant stream of new content. And so it drives ratings by having conversations that don't always reflect an accurate picture of what's happening in the country.

If you want to run a successful news outlet, or a well-read website, I suppose that's how you have to look at politics. But if you want to figure out what's actually happening, and what's likely to come, obsessing over the short term is not the way to do it.

So as you proceed, try not to let the day's events cloud your view of the entire generation to follow.

Instead, take the long view. Think about politics in terms of big-picture trends, think about how dynamics will inevitably change over time. Don't get caught up in the current frenzy, as it'll likely dissipate just as quickly as it appeared. Democrats are not always going to have good days. And they aren't always going to win the battles they fight. But over the long term—even when things might look down, even if the day's news isn't what you were hoping to hear—take the long view. Democrats are about to enjoy unfathomable political advantages. It's already started. Over time, it will just get better. You just have to take a few steps back to see it. And that's where this book comes in.

RULE #2: JUST BECAUSE THE REPUBLICANS WERE WRONG DOESN'T MEAN I AM.

After Bush's reelection in 2004, many prominent Republicans became synonymous with the idea of a permanent majority. At every opportunity, they would celebrate the likelihood that the party could—and would—maintain its control over the federal government for a generation to come.

Fred Barnes, executive editor of the *Weekly Standard*, wrote about the promising future for his cherished GOP in January 2005, not long after Bush's victory.

> Republicans have the presidency and the most senators (55) since 1931, and are near their modern peak in the House (232). They have all but completed the sweeping political realignment they could only dream about a generation ago. In the dark days after the 1964 rout, those dreams seemed quixotic, farfetched, even crazed. Now, they've been realized.

Barnes wasn't the only one anticipating a bright future for the party. "The Republican party is a permanent majority for the future of this country," announced then-House Majority Leader Tom DeLay at his victory party, according to the *Texas Observer*. "We're going to be able to lead this country in the direction we've been dreaming of for years." With Bush reelected, with Republicans in control of government from top to bottom, the future, it seemed, was shifting rightward. Karl Rove reflected on the state of the Democrats in a *New Yorker* profile six months earlier. "I don't think you ever kill any political party. Political parties kill themselves, or are killed, not by the other political party but by their failure to adapt to new circumstances." It was a piece of advice he really should have paid more attention to.

Republicans were indeed in control of the White House and Congress. But the circumstances that were sure to unfold in front of them should have made Karl Rove a permanent majority's biggest skeptic, not its most prominent cheerleader.

Whenever Republicans would discuss the promise of a long-term, durable majority, they were more likely to employ wishful thinking than objective political analysis. They would argue, for example, that Republicans would secure their majority by realigning Hispanic voters with the GOP. They saw the 2004 presidential election results as evidence of that possibility.

But even at their best, Republicans only received 44 percent of the Hispanic vote. Combine that with the strong anti-immigrant feelings expressed on the far right of the party, and Rove should have known better. Sure, if the Hispanic vote had realigned, that would have been great news for the Republican Party. But there was never any real evidence that it had, or ever would. There was just a group of overeager, misinformed conservatives repeating their claims over and over.

This book is not about spin. It's not about wishful thinking. Had GOP strategists looked farther down the road, had they taken into account how demographics were changing in the country, how young people were abandoning the Republican Party, had they actually analyzed the long-term factors that would come into play, they would have seen that it was a Democratic permanent majority on the rise, not a Republican one.

In the end, they were wrong largely because they didn't do the footwork. I have. In the pages that follow, you will learn of the seemingly countless ways in which the Democratic Party is poised to secure a permanent majority. It's all very real and incredibly promising.

RULE #3: YOU CAN SEE A LOT MORE OF THE FUTURE THAN YOU THINK.

There is a lot that we can't predict. Will there be another terrorist attack on American soil? Will the economy fully recover? Will Mike Huckabee eat Mitt Romney? In a world as complex as ours, with a political system as dynamic as ours, it may seem irrational, if not outright wacky, to think that the next generation can be laid out without some kind of heretofore undiscovered magic.

But there is actually quite a bit that we do know. There are events that will unfold—that have to unfold—that will have specific and identifiable consequences. There are trends that show every likelihood of continuing that give us a prism into what lies ahead. This book uses data as a lens to see the future, not as a crystal ball to predict it. All conclusions drawn are based on real facts and real data, not a speculative whim.

RULE #4: IF YOU'RE A REPUBLICAN . . .

Hi. I'm a Democrat. I've worked for Democrats, made donations to Democrats, and written praise of Democrats. You'll see throughout the book that often I will discuss what Democrats need to do to accomplish an objective, and when doing so, I'll use the term *we*. There's no mistaking it. I'm one of them.

That said, there is nothing in this book that isn't relevant to the GOP. I'm a partisan, but I'm an objective partisan. The conclusions I draw are based on the facts on the ground. Those facts don't change whether you fancy yourself red or blue.

Give it a read. But fair warning: It may terrify you. If the Republican leadership doesn't change course soon, our greatest hopes—and your greatest fears—are likely to be realized. On the night he was first nominated on the Democratic presidential ticket, FDR said, "Here and now I invite those nominal Republicans who find that their conscience cannot be squared with the groping and failure of their party leaders to join hands with us." Consider the invitation extended.

RULE #5: HAVE A QUESTION? ASK.

There are a lot of moving parts to building a permanent majority, so if you're reading and you have a question, just ask me on Twitter (@dylanloewe), and I'll get you an answer. In 140 characters, no less. And if you're not sure what I'm talking about, don't worry—just stick with Rules 1–4. They'll get you there just fine.

One last note: Democrats have never had a better opportunity to build a permanent majority. But that doesn't mean they will. There are an exciting number of things that are going in the Democrats' favor that will continue to boost the party over the next quarter century. But there is still plenty that will need to be done—critical actions to be carried out by strong leaders and great presidents. A permanent majority is only won by a party that deserves to win it. The Democrats can build themselves a new progressive era. But only if they get the job done right.

TWO

☆ ☆ ☆

The Escalation of the Fringe

Never interrupt your opponent when he's destroying himself.

—*Paul Begala*

In May of 2009, shortly after President Obama celebrated his one hundreth day in office, *Time* magazine ran a cover story detailing the state of the current Republican Party. The cover displayed an elephant symbol and posed a question:

Is the party over?

The story Michael Grunwald painted inside the magazine was a disturbing picture for a party still reeling from the 2008 election. "These days, Republicans have the desperate aura of an endangered species," Grunwald wrote, describing the challenge the party faces as a "death spiral."

Indeed, through much of 2009, the Republican Party

found itself struggling to stay afloat only a few years after controlling every branch of government. Despite their success, the Republican leadership misread the degree to which the political ground had shifted, however slowly, beneath its feet.

· Back in 2005, the reelected George Bush saw his approval ratings sink to the low forties. A year later, his numbers would crater to levels not recorded since Richard Nixon was forced to resign the presidency. All the while, the public was reassessing and realigning. By the 2006 midterm elections, there would be no turning back.

The leadership of the Republican Party held itself hostage to a far-right ideology; over time, their views became increasingly divorced from those of most Americans. The party lost fifty-two seats in the House between 2006 and 2008 and another fifteen in the Senate. For the once-dominant party, the consecutive losses were devastating. At the presidential level, it was even worse. Obama won every state John Kerry had, plus an additional nine. With the exception of Missouri, the Obama team carried every single battleground state in which it competed.

It was an atmosphere that called for genuine soul searching within the Republican ranks. But those in a position to make those tough choices consistently came up short. Hard as they may have tried, Republican leaders were entirely incapable of engaging in self-reflection—and self-correction. Their postelection postmortem focused predominantly on the belief that the party was led astray, not because it had moved too far to the right, but because, incredibly, it hadn't moved far enough. The party had failed and a wave of Democrats took over the federal government, the GOP concluded, because Republicans just weren't being Republican enough.

While those on the right argued for the same policies using the same talking points that had resulted in such decisive electoral defeats, public polling began to tell a very different story. In April 2009, a Washington Post-ABC News poll found that only 21 percent of Americans identified themselves as Republicans. The next month, Gallup released a survey that found Republican popularity declining among every demographic group imaginable: college graduates, college non-graduates, low income, middle income, upper income, liberal, moderate, conservative, married, unmarried. In fact, the only demographic group in which the Republicans did not decline in popularity was frequent churchgoers.

By October 2009, even as the president's poll numbers began to slide, the national party stayed trapped in its unpopularity: a *Washington Post* poll showed that still only 20 percent of Americans identified themselves as members of the Republican Party.

Through 2009, whatever soul searching occurred didn't appear to produce much tangible value for the party; instead, with their popularity perilously low, Republicans tacked hard to the right, catering almost exclusively to their base.

Dick Cheney quickly emerged as one of the leading voices on the right. In an interview with CNN in March

2009, his first since leaving office, the former vice president appeared to have shed some pounds and perhaps some stress, but he hadn't shed the bitter demeanor and wretched unpleasantness that has come to define his character. He seemed entirely uninterested in conveying the statesmen quality that former executives are so often eager to exude, instead explicitly accusing President Obama of putting the country in harm's way.

"He is making some choices that, in my mind, will, in fact, raise the risk to the American people of another attack," said Cheney, referring to Obama's reversal of a number of Bush administration policies. He expressed similar sentiments in subsequent interviews. In Washington, Democrats rejoiced. If Dick Cheney, one of the most unpopular politicians on the American stage, wanted to elevate himself as chief spokesperson for the opposition, Democrats would welcome it.

But he'd have some strong competition.

In October 2007, Democratic strategists James Carville and Stan Greenberg decided to include Rush Limbaugh in a national poll they were conducting. Finding out Limbaugh was unpopular wasn't all that surprising. But finding out how extraordinarily unpopular he was, especially among young voters, was. With Bush leaving office, the Democrats would need a new enemy and Limbaugh seemed like the ideal figure. He was an egomaniac who thrived on controversy; he'd be easy to bait. Four days before Obama's inauguration, Limbaugh announced that he was hoping for Obama's failure. At the time, it was an

incredibly unpopular sentiment; not only was Obama rid-
ing honeymoon-related sky-high approval numbers, but
the economy was as close as it would ever come to collapsing. Obama's failure would have been the country's failure.

Democrats saw their opening. They began to float the
idea that Limbaugh was the de facto head of the Republican Party. At the same time, the few Republicans who
had been willing to criticize Limbaugh began retracting
and apologizing, adding more fuel to the fire.

Representative Phil Gingrey (R-GA) was among the
first. When asked about Limbaugh in an interview in late
January 2009, he said, "I mean, it's easy if you're Sean
Hannity or Rush Limbaugh or even sometimes Newt Gingrich to stand back and throw bricks. You don't have to
try to do what's best for your people and your party." A
day later, he retracted on Limbaugh's radio show: "I clearly
ended up putting my foot in my mouth on some of those
comments, and I just wanted to tell you, Rush . . . that I
regret those stupid comments."

He wasn't the only one. Though there were a rare few
Republicans willing to take on Limbaugh, each that did
later backed off. Rahm Emanuel and the Democratic establishment couldn't believe their luck. In an appearance on
CBS's *Face the Nation*, Emanuel was asked who he thought
now spoke for the Republican Party. "You just named him:
it's Rush Limbaugh," said Emanuel, not skipping a beat.

He has laid out his vision, in my view. . . . He's not hiding. He's asked for President Obama and called for Pres-

ident Obama to fail. That's his view. And that's what he has enunciated. And whenever a Republican criticizes him, they have to run back and apologize to him and say they were misunderstood. He is the voice and the intellectual force and energy behind the Republican Party.

A few days later, Michael Steele, chairman of the Republican National Committee, decided to enter the fray to counter Emanuel and to make sure people understood that it was Steele who was leader, not Limbaugh. On February 28, 2009, he went on CNN and called Limbaugh an "entertainer," describing his show as "ugly" and "incendiary."

Two days later, on his radio show, Limbaugh struck back.

"You know who needs a little leadership?" Limbaugh asked. "Michael Steele and those at the RNC. I hope the RNC chairman will realize he's not a talking head pundit, that he is supposed to be working on the grassroots and rebuilding it and maybe doing something about our open primary system and fixing it so that Democrats don't nominate our candidates!" Limbaugh shouted. "It's time, Mr. Steele, for you to go behind the scenes and start doing the work that you were elected to do instead of trying to be some talking head media star, which you're having a tough time pulling off."

This was not a time to back down. As chairman of the RNC, Michael Steele actually was a leader of his party. If he, like all the others, went crawling back to Limbaugh to apologize, he'd make the Democrats' argument for them.

Of course, that kind of experiment in rational reasoning was a little too much for Steele. "My intent was not to go after Rush," he shamefully offered later that day in a telephone interview with *Politico*. "I have enormous respect for Rush Limbaugh."

The GOP had been baited, and it bit hard. Limbaugh understood what was happening, but the publicity and the ratings were too good for him to consider stopping. "The administration is enabling me, they are expanding my profile, expanding my audience, expanding my influence," he told *Politico* in a March 2009 e-mail. "An ever larger number of people are now being exposed to the antidote to Obamaism: conservatism, as articulated by me."

It was a win for the Democrats and for Limbaugh, but it was quite damaging for the Republican Party. Even as the story of "Rush as leader" died down, Limbaugh continued to make incendiary comments and was featured so prominently in the news that he dared MSNBC to try going a full week without saying his name. All the while, as the controversy of his comments grew, so did the ranks of Republican politicians who swore to defend him.

The GOP had reached its low point, and some thought rightly that an entirely new strategy was in order.

Enter Eric Cantor, rising star in the GOP leadership and newest face of the Republican Party. Cantor sought headlines as a reformer within the party, as some kind of bold visionary, when he formed the National Council for a New America. He invited other big names in the Republican Party to join him, including Mitt Romney and Jeb Bush.

The idea? A rebranding effort. Back in May of 2008, Tom Davis, an outgoing Republican congressman wrote of his party's brand in a memo to colleagues, "If we were a dog food, they would take us off the shelf." Cantor's group was finally an effort to respond to that unpleasant reality.

"What we're trying to do here today is kick off a series of town hall forums so that we can get back to listening to the people," Cantor told CNN in May 2009.

The first stop was Pie-Tanza, a pizza joint in a strip mall in the suburbs of Washington, D.C. The event got quite a bit of press, but at lunchtime on a Saturday, only seventy-five people showed up.

"It's time for us to listen, first, to learn a little bit, to upgrade our message a little bit, to not be nostalgic about the past because you know things do ebb and flow," offered Jeb Bush, well-aware that the past he was rejecting included the presidencies of his father and brother.

"Listening to people can make a difference," said Mitt Romney at the event. "That's what we're talking about here, we're listening to people."

Outside the restaurant, right-wing protesters slammed the group for suggesting that the party even consider moderating. Some held signs, others ranted against the group for refusing to discuss immigration. Inside, listeners seemed equally skeptical and unconvinced of the need for rebranding at all. "Quite honestly," one questioner told the politicians, "people learn more from listening to Rush Limbaugh's show than in high school or college."

Two days after the meeting, Limbaugh blasted the

council on his radio show. "We do not need a listening tour. We need a teaching tour. That is what the Republican party needs to focus on. Listening tour ain't it." Later, he added, "I'm weary of the same people who drove us to this point telling us what we have to do now. . . . We did it their way in 2008. We did it with the candidate and approach that they thought would work. Pandering. 'We got to listen to the American people.' I maintain that when a politician says we have to listen to the American people and learn, we are pandering. We're not leading."

Same story, different cowardly Republican politician: That Wednesday morning, Cantor appeared on MSNBC's *Morning Joe*. "What do you say to Rush?" asked host Joe Scarborough.

"You know, Joe," Cantor responded, "really, this is not a listening tour."

That first meeting at Pie-Tanza became the last they held. Cantor suspended the group in May 2010, blaming Democrats for its demise. It was a particularly low point for anyone within the GOP who thought that with hard choices, the party might right itself. Instead, it was overtaken in an escalation of the fringe.

It started with whispers early in 2007. Obama is a Muslim. Obama is a secret terrorist. The whispers snowballed into a series of e-mails that mesmerized the right wing. One of the more well-circulated e-mails read, "Since it is politically expedient to be a CHRISTIAN when seeking major public office in the United States, Barack Hussein Obama has joined the United Church of Christ in an attempt to downplay his Muslim background. ALSO, keep in mind that when he was sworn into office he DID NOT use the Holy Bible, but instead the Koran." It continued, "The Muslims have said they plan on destroying the US from the inside out, what better way to start than at the highest level—through the President of the United States, one of their own!!!!"

The rumor campaign served as a backdrop to the 2008 presidential election; the Obama team took a number of steps to combat the false information being disseminated, including the launch of a website called "Fight the Smears." After Obama was elected, those who were expecting the chatter to die down were very much mistaken.

With Obama in the White House, the fringe clung to a favorite meme: Obama isn't really an American, it argued. He was born in Kenya, not Hawaii, and his birth certificate was a fake. What began as a whisper quickly grew into something much more. And as has often been the case in America, when the fringe gets angry, it gets loud.

More and more, stories of birthers began appearing, first on blogs, then in mainstream outlets. Orly Taitz, a lawyer, dentist, real estate agent, leader of the birther movement, and out-of-her-mind crazy person, explained her fears to *Esquire* magazine in August 2009.

I am extremely concerned about Obama specifically because I was born in the Soviet Union, so I can tell that he is extremely dangerous. I believe he is the most dangerous thing one can imagine, in that he represents radical communism and radical Islam: He was born and raised in radical Islam, all of his associations are with radical Islam, and he was groomed in the environment of the dirty Chicago mafia. Can there be anything scarier than that?

Despite its total lack of connection to reality, the birther movement picked up steam in the summer of 2009. A Public Policy Polling survey from September 2009 found that, shockingly, almost half of Republicans believed the president was born outside the United States.

This is where the death spiral comes in. Many of the voters who once would have been seen as traditional Republicans now call themselves Independents. The 20 percent of the country that remained with the party is a more-concentrated brew of the far right—so much so that fully half of them have questions about Obama's citizenship. What inevitably follows? Republican members of Congress start to mimic their constituencies.

Florida Republican Representative Bill Posey authored a piece of legislation that became known as the "Birther Bill," which would require that all future candidates for president provide their birth certificate upon seeking their party's nomination. As Gabriel Winant of *Salon* put it, "Whether it's out of cynicism, fear of the GOP base or simply an inability to read and reason, the ranks of the Birthers in Congress seem to be growing."

Indeed, eleven Republican congressmen signed up as cosponsors to Posey's bill.

When asked about the issue, a number of congressional Republicans raised questions about Obama's birth certificate. Seventeen, in fact. In July 2009, for example, when *Huffington Post* blogger Mike Stark asked Representative Roy Blunt what he thought about Obama's nationality, Blunt responded, "What I don't know is why the President can't produce a birth certificate. I don't know anybody else that can't produce one. And I think that's a legitimate question. No health records, no birth certificate." Two days earlier, Senator Jim Inhofe (R-OK) told *Politico* that birthers "had a point." At a February 2009 town hall in Alabama, Senator Richard Shelby offered this: "Well, his father was Kenyan and they said he was born in Hawaii, but I haven't seen any birth certificate. You have to be born in America to be president." Representative Lynn Jenkins, of Topeka, Kansas, told conservatives at a July 2009 town hall that the GOP would be boosted by "a great white hope" that could thwart Barack Obama and congressional Democrats.

Republican members of Congress are either losing their minds or losing their footing. Or maybe it's both. Either way, with a huge swath of their base foaming at the mouth over conspiracy theories, rather than set the record straight, rather than lead, Republican congressmen moved to the back of the pack.

When Democrats were confronted with a similar fringe, their response was exactly the opposite. On the extreme left, a group of conspiracy theorists emerged who believed that September 11 was perpetrated by the federal government. In October 2007, while Bill Clinton was stumping for his wife's presidential campaign, a protester shouted from the audience, "9/11 was an inside job!"

Clinton paused. "An inside job?" he asked, incredulously. "How dare you!" He paused for effect. "How dare you. It was *not* an inside job." The Democratic audience cheered. "You guys have got to be careful," Clinton continued. "You're going to give Minnesota a bad reputation." For the Democratic Party, that was the only acceptable response to the delusions of that fringe.

The GOP, as it turns out, is an entirely different story. Its members' support of the birther movement might help them survive a primary challenge from the right. But among Independents and Democrats (and among reasonable Republicans), it's a lunacy—an unacceptable, impossible-to-understand craziness born out of hate and fear and outright racism and perpetuated by a party that's proving it doesn't deserve to ever emerge from the depths of minority status.

In the midst of the birthers and all that abject hatred, the "Tea Party" protesters emerged, just in time for the 2009 summer health care debate.

As members of Congress headed home to their districts for the August 2009 recess, the right organized against health care. In town halls held all across the country, anti-reform protesters screamed, yelled, disrupted, and demanded. Stoked by a widespread misinformation campaign, conservatives railed against a government takeover of health care and the evils that would come with it. Republican politicians, seeing a potential opening, brought gasoline by the barrel to the fire. Enter Sarah Palin, who had by then resigned without explanation as governor of Alaska. In August 2009, she wrote on her Facebook page that the health bill was downright evil and that it would create "death panels" that would judge her son Trig, who suffers from Down syndrome, as unworthy.

The comment was rather unsettling—did Sarah Palin really think the health care bill was going to create government-run death panels? She couldn't possibly believe something so impossibly ridiculous—so utterly, entirely insane. But if she didn't believe it, if she made the whole thing up, then she was using her Down syndrome baby as a political prop to sell a lie and drum up fear. So much for family values.

Either way, whether she was selling out her baby or engaging in mindless ramblings, her comments caught on. The town hall meetings that followed came with protesters demanding that representatives vote against a bill that would deem older Americans unworthy of survival. At Senator Ben Cardin's town hall in Maryland, protesters held signs that read, "No to Obama's Death Panels!" A protester at an August 2009 rally in Los Angeles told CBS News, "We didn't stand up when they took prayer out of school and replaced it with drugs, we didn't stand up and we got legalized abortion and they're killing babies, and if we don't stand up now, God help us."

What happened that summer crystallized into a movement—the Tea Party movement—which grew to become the central identity of the American right. Because its mission was unclear, it spokesman nonexistent, the Tea Party movement became a placeholder concept for just about every right-wing philosophy in the spectrum: it was a place for those who believed that health care reform was tantamount to socialism; a place for those with a newfound fear of deficits; a place for pro-life activists and white supremacists—really, a giant family of intolerance and incoherence. But the group was large, almost omnipresent, and very, very loud. It didn't take long for its ideology—and tactics—to creep a bit too far into the halls of Congress.

On September 9, 2009, when Barack Obama addressed a joint session of Congress in an attempt to reset the health care debate, he was booed and heckled by some members of the GOP, most infamously by Representative Joe Wilson, who screamed, "You lie!" at the president, interrupting his speech. It was the perfect contrast for the American people. At the moment when the president was declaring that the time for bickering was over, a representative from the right side of the aisle took the bickering to a new level.

The story of the tea partier crowd is a critical one for the Republican Party. It gave the GOP and many observers the impression that the party wasn't dying, that it was, in fact, being revived. It was mobilizing, acting, influencing the public debate. Tales of Republican demise seemed silly, almost naive.

That feeling became even more pronounced, understandably, when Democrat Martha Coakley lost to Republican Scott Brown in the special election to replace Ted Kennedy in the Senate. Brown had been "endorsed" by the Tea Party and had expressed sympathy for its cause and ideas.

It was an enormous victory for the Republican Party, to be sure. And because it occurred in Massachusetts of all places, it convinced the party that the strategy it had followed for the first year of the Obama presidency had been the right one.

Over time, Republicans will come to find that the lessons they learned were the wrong ones, that their victories in 2009 and 2010 were reflections of temporary circumstances. While the voting public, especially Independents, continues to be frustrated at the slow place of economic recovery, that frustration can certainly translate into unpopular Democrats losing important races. But the economy will recover, and the seething anger so many Americans feel will subside. When it does, the Republicans will find that their strategy did nothing to bridge the gap between the far-right Tea Party crowd they embraced and the sensible people of the rest of the country. The decisions they made in 2009 will haunt them long after 2010.

At a time when the Republican Party should be broadening its appeal by recruiting moderate candidates, the Tea Party crowd says no. Deviation from core principles was deemed unacceptable. And so instead of seeking ways to expand the party, the RNC debated enacting a conservative litmus test for supporting candidates. It included ten categories, from issues like promoting small government and reducing deficits to opposing health care reform, energy reform, immigration reform, and gay marriage. It's a test that even Ronald Reagan and George W. Bush couldn't pass.

As the Tea Party becomes more deeply interwoven into the Republican fabric, moderates will get squeezed out, pushing the GOP even further out of the mainstream. All over the country, moderate Republicans with real appeal to broad constituencies will find themselves mired down in primary challenges from the right. Or worse, they'll find themselves facing a third-party challenge from the right during a general election. That can seriously stifle the hopes of a Republican resurgence. In Nevada for example, Harry Reid, the Senate Majority Leader, began his 2010 reelection campaign with dismal favorability ratings. A number of polls suggested he had little hope of winning in November, making him a prime target for the Republican Party. But in February 2010, the Tea Party qualified to nominate its own candidate to appear on the general election ballot and is threatening to siphon a substantial number of votes from Reid's Republican opponent. That same dynamic will play out in a number of other races during the 2010 election and undoubtedly in congressional elections in the future.

In the short term, the consequences of these problems

are going to remain masked. Democrats are about to lose as many as thirty seats in the House and potentially half a dozen in the Senate, a circumstance that is sure to overshadow the long-term dynamics still at play. But don't let that distract you from the bigger, long-term picture.

Yes, Democrats are about to get trounced in the midterm elections. That's pretty much undeniable. And in reality, not all that surprising. Having been beaten so badly two election cycles in a row, the Republican Party had come close to hitting rock bottom. Meanwhile, Democrats had swollen their ranks dramatically, in districts where Democrats had never won before, districts so conservative that newly elected freshmen were seen as underdogs for reelection from the moment they took office. In a number of cases, members of Congress earned their seats in 2008 based on the unprecedented turnout wave of the Obama campaign. They will now find themselves in an electoral pickle.

Take Tom Perriello, for example. Perriello was a young national security consultant who decided to take on six-term incumbent Republican Virgil Goode in an especially conservative Virginia district. Goode had been the heavy favorite; in 2006 he took 59 percent of the vote, even in the midst of a Democratic takeover.

But by the time Obama had earned the nomination, Virginia had become one of the most critical battleground states of the campaign. A Democrat hadn't won the state since Lyndon Johnson in 1964; but Obama had been polling ahead of McCain for months, and so David Plouffe and the Obama team mobilized a massive effort on the ground. Obama visited Virginia thirty times, more than any other state. The campaign spent tens of millions of dollars there, literally saturated the airwaves with ads. They built a massive infrastructure of volunteers and organized voters in all parts of the state, even in parts as conservative as the district Perriello was running in.

On election day, that surge of support for Obama sent a wave of votes into Perriello's column. By election night, the race was too close to call. A recount was ordered. When Goode finally conceded to the young Democrat, Perriello had won by only 727 votes.

Without the Obama operation going full-tilt in Virginia, Perriello would probably never have made it to Congress. And in 2010, when fewer voters are turning out and with the president's name absent from the ballot, mobilizing enough supporters in such a far-right district may prove to be impossible.

It's the same basic story for a handful of other Democrats of the 111th Congress, freshmen who in 2008 just barely made it to the Democratic Congressional Campaign Committee's (DCCC) coveted "Red to Blue" list and who, on election day, managed to eke out shocking wins in Republican territory largely on the coattails of a historic presidential election.

That dynamic alone would indicate a number of losses for Democrats. But there are other pieces that are creating a perfect storm for the party. The president's party almost always loses in the first midterm elections after he takes office. In fact, Franklin Roosevelt and George W. Bush were the only ones who didn't take that beating. History is not on President Obama's side.

That isn't all that surprising either. Governing isn't easy. When President Obama came into office, the economy was losing 700,000 jobs a month. To save the economy from collapsing in on itself, he had to do some pretty unpopular things: bail out the banks that caused the problem, bail out the auto industry, get Congress to authorize nearly $800 billion to be spent in two years stimulating the economy. By mid-2010, the recession was over, the economy was growing again, the Standard & Poors Index was up more than 70 percent from its low point a year earlier, and job creation was, once again, on the march. But unemployment still remained high, leaving Americans understandably uneasy and Obama without any credit for having prevented the worst from happening.

Some vulnerable Democrats will put up better-than-expected fights in 2010 and win reelection. But others are bound to fall. Still, the Republican Party is unlikely to retake the majority in either chamber—not in these midterms or the ones that will follow.

Fortunately for Democrats, over the course of the next twenty-four years, the 2010 midterms will prove to be the least consequential election. After this race, the congressional maps will be completely redrawn. Democrats may pick up more than a dozen seats from that process alone. All the while, the country's changing demographic landscape will help solidify the Democratic majority over time.

In the meantime, the Republican Party will continue to devolve. Just as they did after Scott Brown's victory, Republicans will see their midterm gains as having validated their strategy of appealing, almost exclusively, to the fringe. These are the wrong lessons to learn and may prove fatal to the GOP's long-term survival.

The impact of the GOP's love affair with the fringe will be far more pronounced over the long term and will start showing its effects in the years that follow the midterms. Over time, the risk of the party becoming significantly insular is not just that it will alienate the rest of the country, but that it will also alienate Republicans who do not identify with the anti-intellectual, anti-fact ranting of the fringe. Richard Posner, an appellate court judge and famous conservative thinker, bemoaned the death of the conservative intellectual. "It is notable that the policies of the new conservatism are powered largely by emotion and religion and have for the most part weak intellectual groundings," he wrote on his blog. "That the policies are weak in conception, have largely failed in execution, and are political flops is therefore unsurprising. . . . By the fall of 2008, the face of the Republican Party had become Sarah Palin and Joe the Plumber. Conservative intellectuals had no party." Many of those leaving the party see the world through eyes not unlike Posner's; when it comes to true conservative thought and sensible economic policies, the GOP is no longer a credible actor.

The Republican Party faces a crisis, the severity of which cannot be overstated. Every strategy decision made by the leaders of the party has suggested that they are either in denial or delusional, incapable of seeing the risks they face over the long term. They are headed off a cliff they cannot see.

If nothing else in the political landscape were changing, the Republican Party would be in terrible shape. But as the chapters that follow will make clear—everything is changing. And it's all moving in the direction of the Democrats. In the time since Obama's inauguration, the Republican Party has indeed failed to adapt and reassess. Instead, it has adopted a political strategy that will only fuel its downfall. An August 2009 Gallup poll found that only four states had a strong Republican advantage in party identification, compared to thirty for Democrats. These numbers will only worsen with time. A permanent majority won't just be handed to the Democrats. But that won't stop the Republican Party from trying.

THREE

☆ ☆ ☆

Where to Draw the Line

As a mapmaker, I can have more of an impact on an election than a campaign, than a candidate.
—David Winston, a Republican political consultant who redrew House seats after the 1990 census

By the end of 2010, the midterms will appear to have been the biggest political story of the year. But the more-important story—the event that will have a broader effect not on one, but on five midterms elections—will have unfolded back in April, not November.

On the first day in that month, the United States officially began conducting the national census.

I know—the census isn't exactly the kind of dramatic political event that makes a front-page headline. But make no mistake about it: The data collected in the census, and the political outcomes that will be based on that data, could help Democrats secure their permanent majority in the House of Representatives.

Here's how it works. Representation in the House is based on population. Of course, our population is constantly changing. So, as mandated by the Constitution, every ten years, the Census Bureau counts the number of people living in the United States. The following year, state legislatures use that new data to redraw the congressional districts in their states, which are required by law to have an even population distribution.

Where there are large increases in population, new congressional districts are added. Where populations are in decline, districts are removed. The outcome is a completely new map, with many districts dramatically redefined. It's a new set of boundaries that will dictate the battle lines of congressional elections for an entire decade.

The reason that's such a big deal for the Democratic Party is that the makeup of the country, in both politics and population, is dramatically different than it was ten years ago. The map that was drawn based on the 2000 census data favored the Republican Party in a number of ways, making it even more impressive that Democrats took back control of Congress in 2006. But the redistricting based on the 2010 census will do just the opposite, reflecting changes in the country that will provide Democrats with a substantial, long-term advantage.

First, let's talk population growth.

Here's something that will warm the heart of any good Democrat. Every place that Democrats are doing well, the population is growing fast. Obama performed great in big cities throughout the country—where populations have been surging over the last decade. He did especially well in midsized cities and put up impressive numbers in the suburbs, where fast-growing populations have shifted the territory from red to blue.

In emerging suburbs, regions that are farther outside the city than traditional suburbs, Obama won a higher percentage of the vote than any Democrat since exit polling first began. Just four years earlier, Bush campaign manager Ken Mehlman described fast-growing suburbs to the *New York Times* as a Republican "fortress." But wins in the suburbs of critical battleground states, including Pennsylvania, Michigan, Ohio, Florida, Virginia, and North Carolina, were, in large part, the product of Obama's strength in their suburban regions. Simply put, everywhere America is growing, it is also liberalizing. And the places where America is growing are most likely to gain additional congressional seats after census results come in.

Think about what that can mean for redistricting. Population growth is at the center of the changes that will be made to the congressional map. And across the board, in parts of the country that are growing the fastest, in those places most likely to gain new House seats, Democrats are seeing huge surges of support. That will surely mean new congressional districts will be created in places where Democrats can—and will—win.

But geographic growth isn't the only factor fueling that charge for more Democratic House seats. Demographics are also playing an exceptionally important role.

Much of the Democrats' new geographic dominance is

the product of substantial increases in minority populations. Minorities made up a staggering 80 percent of the
U.S. population growth between 2000 and 2010. By 2042,
the United States is projected to have minorities make up
a majority of its population. This is a big deal for Democrats. During the twenty years between Michael Dukakis's defeat and Obama's victory, the minority share of
voters increased by nearly 75 percent. And on election
day 2008, a staggering 80 percent of minorities voted
for Obama. Minorities are the most loyal bloc of progressive voters, and they are the country's fastest-growing
population.

At the same time that the Democratic populace is expanding, the Republican coalition is experiencing a dangerous shrinking. John McCain's voters were an incredibly
narrow bunch. They were predominantly rural and
working-class voters, mostly concentrated in parts of
Appalachia and the Deep South that are aging and con-
tracting in size. Over 90 percent were white. The fright-
ening bottom line for the GOP is that Republican
strongholds are getting smaller, and Republican voters
are dying off.

Ruy Teixeira drove the point home in "New Progressive America," a March 2009 report from the Center for
American Progress. Over the last twenty years, "the
minority share of voters in presidential elections has risen
by 11 percentage points, while the share of increasingly
progressive white college graduate voters has risen by four
points. But the share of white working-class voters, who

have remained conservative in their orientation, has plummeted by 15 points."

Over the long term, that will only worsen. As Teixeira notes, the Hispanic population "will triple to 133 million by 2050—from 47 million today—while the number of non-Hispanic whites will remain essentially flat. Moreover, as a percentage of the population, Hispanics will double from 15 percent to 30 percent." With voting populations changing that dramatically, Republicans can expect to lose House seats across the country. And the bad news doesn't end there.

During the last redistricting, the Republican Party was the dominant force in politics at the state level. With the GOP in charge, gerrymandering was the name of the game. Take Texas, for example.

In 2003, after Republicans took control of all branches of Texas state government, the legislature attempted to ram a redistricting plan through. The map, designed by Tom Delay and other prominent Republicans, was one of the most outwardly political redistricting plans in American history.

It erased the seats of two Democratic members of Congress. Other members saw their districts morphed and mutilated, designed to be too conservative for a Democrat to possibly win. Liberal areas were sliced out, conservative areas squeezed in. An excited Republican operative, on reading the redistricting plan, sent an internal e-mail to other staffers that was later published by the Texas politics blog *Burnt Orange Report:* "The maps are now official. I have studied them and this is the most aggressive map I have ever seen. This has a real national impact that should assure that Republicans keep the House no matter the national mood." He wasn't entirely right. Funny what an unpopular war and a bad economy can do to the national mood. Still, the map was truly devastating. Democrats stood to loose five—perhaps six—seats, perhaps more.

Hoping to prevent the new redistricting plan from being voted on, a few Democratic state house members hatched a plan: State law requires that business on the floor of the state house only be conducted when a quorum of two-thirds of its members are present. If 51 of the 150 Texas house members left town, it would literally shut the state house down, preventing it from, among other things, voting on the Republican plan. With no other viable option, that's just what the Democrats did.

Hugh Brady, the Democratic caucus's chief of staff, placed a call to the Ardmore Holiday Inn in Oklahoma, reserving twenty-six rooms in his name. Under cover of darkness, state legislators piled into two chartered buses in which neither driver was aware of the final destination. When fifty-one were accounted for, they snuck across Texas, heading north. They arrived at the hotel six hours later.

Governor Rick Perry freaked out. He ordered the legislators to return or be arrested. He even sent the Texas Rangers after them, hoping to find that they were hiding somewhere in Texas. When it was discovered that they were in Oklahoma, beyond the jurisdiction of the Rangers,

Tom Delay got involved at the federal level. He called the Department of Homeland Security and tried, unsuccessfully, to get the FBI to intervene. Texas Republicans had been outwitted. The Democrats did not return until the legislative session had expired.

It wasn't the first time in history that blocking a quorum was used as a legislative tactic. Abraham Lincoln and some of his fellow state legislators actually jumped out of a window in Springfield to prevent a vote. It didn't work. In 1988, Republicans walked out of the Senate to prevent the passage of a campaign finance bill. That didn't work, either. Capitol police literally dragged Senator Bob Packwood back into the chamber—feet first. Blocking a quorum almost never works—it certainly hasn't through history. And as Texas Democrats would soon find out, it had worked for them only temporarily.

Back in Austin, Republicans pressed on, undeterred. In August, the governor called a special legislative session for the sole purpose of getting a vote on the redistricting plan. This time, it was the state senators who would leave town.

Eleven Democratic state senators chartered two private jets to New Mexico, where they would try to wait out the session. They were escorted, upon arrival, by the New Mexico state police, who had heard rumors that Texas might send authorities into New Mexico after them. They would have to stay there for thirty days, until the special session expired. That prospect was easier for some of the senators to stomach than others. The eleven received national attention for their unorthodox political tactic, but with such attention came political pressure. They held strong for twenty-two days until, one morning, State Senator John Whitmire buckled under the strain and returned to Texas, where he vowed to fight redistricting from the Senate floor. Many suspect he made a deal with Republicans. He was the only additional senator they would need to finally achieve their quorum. His departure left no reason for the other ten senators to remain on the lam. It was a crushing betrayal. Days later, just before the end of the special session, the redistricting plan was passed. In the next year's congressional election, six Democrats lost their seats.

Republicans controlled the process in Texas back then. They controlled it in Michigan, too, where a Republican-controlled legislature orchestrated a gerrymandering that pitted six Democratic congressmen against one another.

But in 2011, when state legislatures convene to redistrict anew, it's the Democrats who will be mostly in control across the country. In 2001, Democrats had majority control in the state legislatures of just sixteen states. After the 2008 election, they had twenty-seven. If they hold their own in the 2010 gubernatorial races, they will have much greater control over the process than they did ten years ago. The political backlash that powered the 2006 and 2008 elections had as notable an impact on state-level government, swelling the ranks of Democrat-controlled legislatures. During the last three election cycles, Democrats saw a net increase of 374 state House seats and 68 state Senate seats around the country. In the end, that advantage will help undo the ubiquitous inequities built into the system by the Republican Party and will ultimately guarantee more Democrats in Congress.

Add all those pieces together and you have a recipe for Democrats picking up as many as a dozen seats—maybe more—on redistricting alone.

What does that mean for the permanent majority? For the next decade, it puts Democrats in a much stronger position to keep control of the House. There will be far more safe Democratic seats added to the Congress; it can also shift other districts leftward, helping make Republican seats vulnerable and tough Democratic seats safer. Make no mistake about it. As a result of the 2010 census, the inequities of the last decade will be righted, and the Democratic Party will solidify its control of Congress.

And things just get better in 2020.

First, the demographic changes that influenced the 2010 census will be that much more pronounced ten more years down the line. Urban growth is expected to continue at an increasingly fast pace, as is the population of minority communities.

Second, and perhaps more dramatic, the 2020 census can be the first in American history to use sampling, a statistical technique at the heart of a longstanding battle between Republicans and Democrats.

Here's the problem: As the census works now, surveys are mailed to individual households and census workers go door to door to do a literal head count of the 310 million people in the country. The problem with that kind of count is that it misses millions of people every time we try it. We've gotten better over time, but still, in 1990, the Census Bureau estimates it missed 8 million people and counted 4 million people twice. In 2000, 2.7 million people were overlooked. Those aren't just numbers. Americans who are not counted in the census are not fully represented in Congress.

To fix the problem, the Census Bureau can introduce a statistical process called sampling. After the bureau does the initial census, it does another, smaller count of a representative sample of people (hence, "sampling"). It's the same as the idea behind a public opinion poll, but instead of calling a few hundred people and getting a result with a substantial margin of error, sampling requires that another 300,000 to 500,000 people be surveyed, creating an extremely accurate result.

Republicans are not interested in an accurate result. Though that may seem irrational, it's actually rooted in political survival. As it turns out, the vast majority of those who are undercounted by the census are minorities and the urban poor, groups that overwhelmingly support the Democratic Party. If they were accurately counted, it would create a substantial number of new House seats in Democratic areas. It would help reveal a more liberal America and would serve as the basis for a further expansion of the Democratic majority. For that reason,

Republicans have battled in the past, and will continue to battle in the future, to make sure that the census continues to produce a faulty result.

They've been pretty successful in that battle, too. Adding sampling into the census costs money, and that requires an appropriation from Congress, usually by mid-decade. In the mid-1990s, Republicans controlled Congress, so they made sure that no appropriation would be made for the purpose of adding sampling into the 2000 census. Same deal in 2004 and 2005, when Republicans controlled all branches of government. That's why we didn't get sampling into the 2010 census.

But if the Democrats are in control of Congress in 2015, Robert Groves, the census director—and sampling expert—will be able to get his appropriation. In 2020, with a Democratic president and Democrat-controlled Congress, sampling can become a reality for the first time.

This could be a game changer, laying some of the most critical foundation for securing a permanent majority. Millions of minorities were left out of the last census count; by 2020, millions more will have entered the population. For the first time in history, they will be counted accurately and represented fairly. A census tempered by sampling will mean Democrats could pick up another five to ten more seats. If the House of Representatives is made to reflect the true makeup of the country, a more liberal America will undoubtedly emerge.

All of this promise can help bring about a generational

Democratic majority in Congress. But to ensure that it comes to fruition, Democrats need to be prepared; they'll need to take action immediately.

Now that the 2010 census has been administered, Democrats must be prepared for a battle that will include political grappling in state legislatures and aggressive litigation whenever and wherever necessary. For the first time since the Voting Rights Act was passed, the attorney general that will enforce the act, Eric Holder, was appointed by a Democratic president. That will give the party a unique opportunity to protect the interests of minority voters. The party must also fight a national public relations war with the GOP, all as Republican candidates gear up to challenge Obama's reelection. But as Democrats push their fight, they must avoid being perceived as playing politics with democracy. By its nature, redistricting is unavoidably and undeniably political. Politicians with vested interests in the outcome of newly drawn maps are the same politicians who get to draw those maps. It feels organically undemocratic, like a vestige from a primitive political era, and one used now only as a vehicle for corruption and manipulation. If Democrats seek to use the power of redistricting to provide themselves with an advantage as inequitable to Republicans as the current map is to Democrats, they will do so with great risk. They must avoid even the appearance that they are pushing to politicize the process, or they could be handing the GOP a potent talking point.

Instead, Democrats must concentrate on correcting past wrongs. Republicans will try to portray Democrats as politically opportunistic, motivated by increasing their power rather than fixing past inequities. Democrats should take that debate head on. To win, they will have to appear honest and fair—more concerned about the accuracy of the process than its outcome. President Obama must be a leading voice in that argument.

Given the critical role that state legislatures will play in the long-term security of the Democratic majority, national Democrats should also dedicate significant financial and organizational resources to state-level elections in 2010. In states like Tennessee, for example, Democrats have a chance to retake control of the state house. Doing so will almost definitely have an impact on the redistricted map the legislature produces in 2011. Gubernatorial races will be critical as well, as governors have the authority to veto a redistricted map. More than half of the thirty-nine governorships that will be up for election will be open-seat races. The outcome of those races will dictate much of the redistricting process.

But in addition to offense, Democrats must maintain a defensive posture in critical states. New York, Virginia, and Louisiana, among others, face statewide vulnerabilities for Democrats. Democrats must be willing to make serious investments in state-level campaigns at a time when all eyes will be on the congressional midterms, recognizing that the potential impact of state-level races could net more congressional seats than the midterms themselves.

In Texas, for example, if Democrats play their cards right, they'll have a chance to reverse Tom DeLay's redistricting nightmare. In the 2008 election, Texas Democrats clawed back into contention in the state house and are now only two seats away from wresting majority control from the Republicans. If Democrats can retake the state house in 2010, it will set up a legislative and judicial showdown around redistricting. The Texas state constitution requires the legislature to produce a redistricting plan after new federal census data is made available. But should the legislature be unable to come to agreement on a plan, the federal courts must intervene to draw the new map. This happened in 2001, when Democrats still held the state house and prevented the Republican-drawn map from passing.

If Democrats can retake the state house in 2010, it could happen again. And if not the state house, the governor's mansion could work, too. Bill White, who enjoyed 80 percent approval ratings while mayor of Houston, is running the most credible Democratic campaign for governor that Texas has seen since Ann Richards. If he wins, he can veto a redistricting plan, sending the process to the courts. If that happens, a federal court will draw the new map based on a set of criteria it defined when it had to do the same thing ten years earlier. The court will first redraw the majority-minority districts. Each of those are Democrat-controlled and cannot be modified by law. Then the court will add a projected three to four new seats onto the map based on where population increases are most abundant. As with the rest of the country, those population increases are in large metropolitan areas that are trending Democratic. A neutral court that draws districts over these populations is likely to produce several more Democratic seats. Next, the court will remove and redraw districts that have been gerrymandered into what it describes as "patently bizarre" shapes. Most of the Democrats who lost their seats after the DeLay redistricting lost them because of the bizarre shapes DeLay created. When the court takes this step alone, it may restore as many as five additional Democratic seats.

In total, a neutral map would mean a net gain of seven to ten seats for Democrats in Texas, a staggering result to come out of a single state. If Democrats want to help secure a permanent majority in the House of Representatives, they'd be wise to invest as many resources as available in the Texas state house races and Bill White's campaign.

Once the 2010 census results have been fully incorporated into the 2011 redistricting plan, it will be time for Obama to look to 2020. He will have to push aggressively for statistical sampling to be included within the 2020 census, regardless of the political pressure he will likely face. That he has named Robert Groves as his census director is an excellent start, to be sure, but it will require legitimate follow-through.

By 2014, Groves needs to be given a green light. He'll need to have a plan in place and have requested that Congress appropriate funds to get the job done. It's a big job.

In addition to counting roughly 300 million Americans, it will require a statistically precise measurement of another half a million individuals. The administration would be wise to proceed with care, but for a permanent Democratic majority to have its best shot, it will ultimately have to act aggressively to ensure that sampling is fully utilized.

Let's recap: Democrats currently hold a seventy-seven-seat majority in a House of Representatives where districts were drawn largely by Republicans based on numbers that undercounted Democrats. Since that time, Democratic voting populations have grown dramatically and Democrats have taken control of a majority of the state legislatures that will make redistricting decisions.

And a new census, packed with good news for Democrats, was just recently administered.

Redistricting holds the key to establishing a permanent majority in the House of Representatives. Last time around, Republicans drew districts all over the country that were specifically designed to make elections more difficult for Democrats; but Democrats rose to the challenge. Districts that were designed to be safe Republican seats fell to Democrats in the West, the Midwest, the Northeast, and the South. And it will only get easier from here.

The idiosyncrasies drawn into districts to make them artificially conservative can be erased. Democratic voters overloaded into urban districts will be more equitably distributed, making conservative districts more competitive.

Democrats in tough districts will find reelection less difficult. Republicans in what were once considered safe seats will find themselves unaccustomed to their new-found political vulnerability.

The 2011 redistricting process could be responsible for bringing in as many new Democrats into the House as a successful midterm election cycle. But unlike the land-slides of 2006 and 2008, redistricting gains are likely to result in more liberals in Congress rather than more mod-erates. With the current congressional map, the DCCC succeeded in 2006 and 2008 largely by recruiting moder-ate Democrats who could compete deep in Republican ter-ritory. When they were elected, the number of centrist Democrats in Congress swelled considerably. But new seats added to states based on population growth in urban areas are likely to be safe Democratic seats, ones where more-progressive candidates, among them many minori-ties, can get elected.

The American population is changing. Quickly. Every-where it's growing, Democrats are doing well. Everywhere Republicans have succeeded, populations have declined. There are other changes, too. The way we count people and the way we provide them with representation is chang-ing. As the country becomes more populated with pro-gressives, the tools to count them accurately and to reflect them honestly in our population can be used for the first time. It's a one-two punch for Democrats. The millions who fueled record population growth will be included in the new redistricting plan. The millions who are undercounted, who are continually kept hidden, can be included in the next one. Both groups are overwhelmingly Democratic and can help change the congressional landscape by electing new Democrats to newly drawn districts throughout the next two decades.

By 2012, the newly drawn map will put Democrats in their strongest position to secure a permanent majority in the party's history, and it will be timed to coincide perfectly with Barack Obama's reelection.

FOUR

☆ ☆ ☆

The Four-Year Head Start

They talk about key people in the states. What key people?
Don't they realize that the day of the organization is
over?

> —*Kenneth O'Donnell, in 1967, while making*
> *preparations for Bobby Kennedy's presidential*
> *campaign*

It wasn't until March of 2007 that anyone started paying attention to the Obama organization. He'd announced his candidacy about six weeks earlier, fueling excitement among supporters and curiosity among journalists. How he would take on Hillary Clinton and the political machine she and her husband had built over more than two decades was unclear. He'd given speeches at rallies, held town halls, drummed up plenty of positive media coverage. But in March, the campaign was still in its infancy; Obama hadn't even debated yet.

March 31 was a filing deadline with the Federal Election Commission. Presidential candidates, for the first time, would have to disclose how much they had raised over the previous quarter, a critical metric for judging the viability of a candidacy. The conventional wisdom was that Hillary Clinton would raise an unprecedented sum and would hold far and away the most cash on hand among all the candidates.

The deadline came and went. The next day, the Clinton campaign announced its numbers. Clinton had raised a record $26 million, which, according to the *Washington Post,* was "almost three times as much as any politician has previously raised at this point in a presidential election." Clinton's campaign manager told the *Post* that they had far exceeded their expectations.

For days, the media devoured the story; what better proof could there be of the inevitable juggernaut that was the Clinton candidacy? All the while, the Obama team remained quiet, letting the media build up the significance of the story. Then, midweek, Obama's team made its announcement.

Barack Obama had raised a whopping $25 million. The lede in the *New York Times* said it all: "If there was any doubt that Senator Barack Obama could stand toe to toe with Senator Hillary Rodham Clinton, at least in raising money, the matter was settled on Wednesday. . . ." The news for Obama just got better from there. Clinton's campaign had refused to disclose how much of the money raised was designated for the primary (candidates could raise money for the primary campaign and the general election, but they could only use the funds for the general election if they won the nomination). When the Clinton

campaign finally disclosed the number, the Obama campaign learned that it had outraised the Clinton campaign
for the primary by almost $6 million.

There was no mistaking it—Barack Obama was the
real deal.

How did he do it? It was the question on the mind of
every political observer not intimately involved with the
inner-workings of the campaign. How was it possible that
this freshman senator with no national list, with no
national infrastructure, could out-raise the best political
machine in Democratic politics? It seemed absolutely impossible.

Then came the unprecedented crowds. More than
20,000 people greeted Obama in Austin. Another 20,000
in Atlanta, 10,000 in Iowa City, and 24,000 in New York
City. What was happening? It was obvious that Obama was
inspiring hundreds of thousands of people, but how was he
also moving them to participate so actively in the process?

Though Obama campaign officials desperately tried to
avoid it, the campaign was inevitably compared to the
Howard Dean model of four years earlier. He, too, could
excite large crowds; he, too, could raise money on the
Internet. But in Iowa, when it came time to caucus, the
voters Dean had counted on never showed up. For many
in the media, the Obama campaign—the elusive Obama
operation—seemed destined to follow a similar path.

Before Iowa, it was impossible to really know for sure.
But by October 2007, *Politico*'s Roger Simon started to notice something interesting—something that suggested

the campaign organization was more than just smoke and mirrors. Simon wrote, "Barack Obama began his speech in an odd and important way, a way that did not make a single news story."

Obama had opened his speech not with hope, but with logistics. "If you have not yet signed up as a Barack Obama supporter, hopefully after the speech you will. Fill out one of those cards. We'll have volunteers all across the doors. You won't be able to get out without seeing one of these cards."

It was community organizing at its most basic, further proof that the Obama team was building something real. The Obama campaign clearly understood the rules of the game: Mobilizing folks to caucus on a snowy January night in Iowa was about banking voters—identifying supporters and making sure the operation was big enough to bring them out of their houses. This wasn't just being fueled by new technologies; it was being orchestrated by a massive field operation made up of scores of twenty-somethings frantically knocking on doors, working eighteen-hour days for $2,000 a month—all in pursuit of signing up supporters. Still, there were questions. The organization on the ground was larger in scope than any that had come before it, but would it really make a difference?

Journalists continued to wonder. Then, at Senator Tom Harkin's steak fry in September, an Iowa political tradition that's an informal metric of candidate support, Obama arrived best organized of all. In addition to giant signs held by supporters, Obama entered the venue flanked and followed by thousands of supporters, chanting and cheering. Observers took note.

At the Jefferson Jackson dinner, another political staple of the Iowa campaign, all the major Democratic candidates were invited to speak. The Obama campaign organized a crowd so large and enthusiastic that, despite it being an event for all candidates, the night often took on the feeling of an Obama-inspired rock concert—as if he'd already secured the nomination. That night, when he spoke, he did so with a new speech and a new fire as thousands cheered. The energy of that excitement elevated his performance. It went over so well that he took the speech to the stump.

As January 3 arrived, with polls showing a tight, three-person race, the question of whether Obama's operation could get the job done would finally be answered.

Around 8:30 P.M. in Iowa, MSNBC called the race. Barack Obama had confounded expectations, winning the caucus by eight points. His operation and his candidacy were indeed something different—the win was proof that the movement Obama had created could very well propel him to the White House. The culmination of the campaign's efforts on that day was only the first in what would be a series of historic and dramatic victories. What Obama and his team built, what they accomplished was incalculably large. And it all began with the simple, but critical vision of the mild-mannered campaign manager.

David Plouffe had long understood the importance of organizing. He was a long-time field operative who specialized in building operations to mobilize voters to the polls (though he'd never done a presidential campaign). After the experience of the 2004 campaign, Plouffe had clearly understood the promise of integrating a sophisticated Internet operation into a campaign's infrastructure.

In early 2007, Plouffe hired Joe Rospars to build the campaign's entire Internet operation. Rospars had been one of the key members of Howard Dean's new media campaign and had founded Blue State Digital, a new media firm, with three other former Dean staffers in early 2004. Rospars would become new media director, setting up shop in the Obama campaign's Chicago headquarters.

With his decision, Plouffe decided to buck the trend of other campaigns. The idea of having a new media director on a campaign was, in itself, a relatively novel idea. Before 2004, the concept of the position didn't even exist. Even in 2008, most down-ballot campaigns operated without one. But Plouffe took the idea one step further. Of those campaigns that had a position dedicated to new media, the campaign structure usually had the new media director answering to a number of department heads, including the field director, communications director, and finance director. But Plouffe didn't want his operation run that way. He wanted Rospars reporting directly to him, making new media its own department and placing Rospars on equal footing with other directors.

The next step was hiring the best new media people the campaign could find. The campaign brought on Chris Hughes, the baby-faced twenty-two-year-old founder of Facebook, to play a key role in the new media team. It hired a graphic designer who had been creative director at a top ad agency. Its chief technology officer had been the founding CIO of Orbitz, the popular travel website. By the time they were fully staffed, the new media team alone was eighty-one members strong, many of whom were at the forefront of the Web 2.0 revolution.

The goal was simple. Barack Obama had the ability to inspire millions; the new media team would need to harness that power and build a mechanism that could raise hundreds of millions of dollars, communicate the campaign's message to millions of people online, and mobilize voters to the polls—especially new voters—in unprecedented numbers. In short, they'd have to put together a political apparatus that would be more expansive and sophisticated than any in the history of American politics.

And they'd have to do it from scratch.

Well, not entirely from scratch. They were starting with Barack Obama as their candidate—the guy who could take a speech in 2004 and turn it into a presidential campaign in 2008, the guy who had inspired so much excitement among his early supporters that opposing campaigns joked about a Kool-Aid–drinking cult forming. In the first twenty-four hours after Obama announced his candidacy, more than 1,000 volunteer groups had been created on the campaign website. There was no mistaking it—Barack Obama was not your average candidate.

Obama was the X-factor for the organization. The system they'd build would be substantial and efficient, but the scope of its success would be deeply embedded in the candidate's ability to continue to inspire. The drill was simple: Campaign staffers would announce an upcoming rally; an army of volunteers would get the word out; targeted e-mails would be sent out; thousands would show up to hear Obama speak. Then, scores of volunteers would flank the crowd, collecting e-mail addresses and other contact information. Those new e-mail addresses would be used to generate even more folks to the next event. More people. More e-mail addresses. Rinse. Repeat. Rinse. Repeat.

The list they'd put together would be the centerpiece of fundraising and field operations. It was how fundraising e-mails would reach small donors, how new information and important talking points could be disseminated to vocal supporters, and how volunteers would be identified and mobilized.

According to Obama Field Director Jon Carson, the campaign obsessed over testing the functionality of everything it did on the Internet and how it would impact the ground game offline. On June 9, 2007, seven months before the Iowa caucus, the Obama campaign sought to test whether or not it could use its still very new online operation to mobilize supporters in Iowa. In the weeks leading up to the test event campaign members named "Walk for Change," volunteers and field staff organized online volunteer groups, mobilized supporters from neighboring states, coordinated buses to key cities, and worked out supporter housing arrangements for anyone coming to Iowa for the weekend. On the campaign website, Regional Field Director Ray Rivera led a training session in canvassing door-to-door, giving basic advice to the volunteers who would be handing out Obama campaign literature. When the day finally arrived, 10,000 volunteers spread out across Iowa, carrying with them Obama's message—and proof to the staff in Chicago that their operation had wings.

At the center of that operation was the campaign website my.barackobama.com, nicknamed "MyBo" by the staff. MyBo was essentially a set of tools, a slew of ways that voters could interact on an individual level with the campaign and with the Obama community. Someone who signed onto the site could learn more about the candidate, either by reading his positions or watching the scores of Obama-related videos made available. They could sign up to receive more information, create a user profile on the site, write a blog, read a blog, register to vote, create a personal fundraising page, join volunteer groups, create volunteer groups, RSVP to local events, and on, and on, and on. If there was a way to interact, it could be done with MyBo.

It was extraordinarily successful as a fundraising tool. According to "Online Tactics & Success," a comprehensive report on the Obama campaign developed by M+R Strategic Services for the Wilburforce and Brainerd foundations, the campaign sent out more than 350 e-mails to supporters—though never more than three to a single supporter in a single day. Some were direct fundraising pleas, others were requests for volunteers. Some were used to transmit important information, video messages from the candidate, or responses to attacks. And much of the e-mail campaign was a key tool for rapid response.

As the Wilburforce report explained, the campaign's ability to use its organization as a tool to react to negative press was impressive. "Nothing exemplifies the importance of nimbleness better than the 'community organizer' email sent by David Plouffe on the night of the Republican Convention," the report explains. In her speech that night, Sarah Palin had mocked Barack Obama's time as a community organizer, and in doing so, had insulted the organized community the Obama campaign had built. Plouffe saw a perfect opportunity. His e-mail opened with him telling supporters, "I wasn't planning on sending you something tonight." The e-mail that was sent out that night "contained a modest request for a $5 donation to help 'remind [the McCain campaign] that everyday people have the power.'" That e-mail alone raised $11 million for the campaign.

The campaign also experimented with other innovative ways to build lines of communication with potential supporters. When Obama was poised to name his vice presidential nominee, the campaign sent out an e-mail to supporters, telling them they could sign up to be the first to know who Obama's pick would be—via text message. Thousands provided their phone numbers to the campaign. At every opportunity, the new media team was looking for new ways to make contact with supporters. The text message effort had proved especially worthwhile;

according to the Wilburforce report, on election day, supporters in precincts where long lines had formed or where glitches had slowed the voting process got critical text messages from the campaign: "Stay in line! The polling hours are being extended to be sure everyone gets to vote!" By then, the campaign had collected over 3 million text-message-capable numbers.

The scope of the operation was incredibly expansive. The return on investments made was extraordinary. Sending a single e-mail would cost the campaign essentially nothing. It took a short period of time and required minimal staff input. And, because so many participated in the arduous process of building a rich campaign list, the campaign could bring in dramatic amounts of money, all from a click of the "send" button.

Through the same operation, it could mobilize the field program, too. Field organizers could recruit volunteers, targeting specific supporters for specific purposes. They could use the operation to register voters—through a site the campaign set up called Vote for Change, 700,000 voters downloaded voter registration forms. "In a number of primary states," the Wilburforce report notes, "the number of voter registration forms downloaded exceeded the margin of victory."

In the end, the operation was extraordinarily successful. According to Blue State Digital, the campaign raised over $750 million from over 3 million donors. Six and a half million donations were made online, making up two-thirds of all the money raised by the campaign. Through personal fundraising pages, 70,000 individuals raised $30 million. And the average online donation was only $80.

In terms of new media success, the campaign ended with a 13 million person e-mail database. It banked over 2 million social networking participants on MyBo and 3.4 million Facebook supporters. Using MyBo tools, participants organized 200,000 events across the country, wrote 400,000 blog entries, and created 35,000 volunteer groups.

According to Blue State Digital, in the last four days of the campaign, supporters used MyBo tools to make 3 million phone calls to voters. And in terms of video content, voters spent 14 million hours watching over 1,800 Obama campaign-related videos.

In total, the campaign spent $250 million in television ads, enough money to saturate the airwaves—enough, indeed, to preempt network primetime with a thirty-minute Obama campaign infomercial in October.

As Plouffe notes in his campaign memoir, *The Audacity to Win,*

> Our e-mail list had reached 13 million people. We had essentially created our own television network, only better, because we communicated directly with no filter to what would amount to about 20 percent of the total number of votes we would need to win—a remarkably high percentage. And those supporters would share our positive message or response to an attack, whether through orchestrated campaign activity like door

knocking or phone calling or just in conversations they had each day with friends, family, and colleagues.

What had first been little more than an abstraction, a vision for a new kind of campaign, snowballed into an unstoppable force, half hope and half juggernaut, the best-funded, best-executed campaign in American history.

The Obama new media team performed flawlessly; they deserve much of the credit for Obama's victory in 2008. But the groundwork they laid—the operation they built and maintained, tested and retested, reshaped and perfected—is about more than that single campaign. The Obama Internet story is important to the permanent majority not because of what was temporarily built, but because of what was left behind.

For starters, the operation left that giant 13 million person e-mail list behind. It's hard to overstate the value of this database. Let's put it in perspective: Hillary Clinton, who started her presidential campaign with an unmatched political machine and who ran an aggressive campaign online, ended her campaign with a 2.5 million member e-mail list. Four years earlier, John Kerry ended his campaign with 3 million. Howard Dean's list numbered only 600,000.

But size isn't everything. The quality of a list can determine its effectiveness as much as its quantity can. When ranking this type of database, *Politico* reporter

Kenneth Vogel described criteria often used by political strategists to assess a list's value. In addition to size, the criteria include "freshness, comprehensiveness (does it include addresses, land lines, cell phone numbers or donation data?), open rates (what percentage of emails in a given send get opened), click-throughs (how many links are activated), actions and donations (how many emails result in a contribution or letter to a member of Congress), as well as intangibles like buzz and list managers' skills."

By all accounts, Obama's list is the best in each category. It is incredibly fresh, organically built, and remarkably rich with data. Names and e-mail addresses are connected to cell phone numbers and social network profiles, with detailed donor history and campaign participation levels noted.

In the past, one of the challenges that both parties have faced is how to turn the organizational investments made by a successful campaign into something of tangible value after election day. Usually, most of the political apparatus that is laid down during a campaign disappears entirely by year's end. Field staffers go home. Offices close. Volunteers go back to their day jobs.

With a list like Obama's, that political operation can remain intact—at least virtually. That information is still available, still accessible, still capable of being utilized. Participants can still be easily contacted and interacted with. Information can continue to be updated. In order to do just that—to keep that list fresh and active, to nurture it, to ensure that the campaign's most-ardent supporters remain engaged—the Obama campaign transformed itself after the election into a Democratic Party project called Organizing for America (OFA).

At first, the fledgling organization was unsure how to best utilize the list. The organization was criticized for early offers to sell commemorative Obama gear (from mugs to photo albums to calendars). Eventually, the president directed the organization to rally behind the Democratic legislative agenda, and, soon, the organization found its voice.

When conservatives rushed town hall meetings during the 2009 health care debate, OFA responded by rallying its members to show up to meetings in support of health care reform. They scheduled a strategy conference call with the president that people could call into or listen to online. The Democratic National Committee reported that 270,000 participated in the call. And in 2010, during the final ten-day run-up to the health care bill finally passing, OFA orchestrated over 500,000 phone calls to Congress. According to Ari Melber of the *Nation*, "The group also executed over 1,200 events during that period, about 100 per day, and mobilized a novel program for over 120,000 supporters to call other Obama fans in key districts to fan local enthusiasm for the bill—a first for either national party." That kind of effort, and the pressure it created for waffling Democratic candidates, could have easily been responsible for the health care bill's ultimate passage. In every way, the organization has continued to build where the campaign left off. It now has about 4 million followers on Twitter, making the organization one of the most visible on that website.

Organizing for America will surely continue to evolve over time. As the first organization of its kind, it does not have the luxury of a user's manual. As its leaders experiment to determine which campaign techniques are most effective in a governing context, we can expect them to fall short at times. But, undoubtedly, the operation has the potential to be a potent weapon for the Democratic Party. Over the long term, it may well become the central piece of the party's organizational force.

From within the White House, the president also continued to provide the same kinds of community tools he used during the campaign to connect Americans to his administration. Valerie Jarrett, one of the president's most trusted senior advisers, was appointed to oversee the White House Office of Public Engagement and Intergovernmental Affairs. The goal, according to whitehouse .gov, is to "create and coordinate opportunities for direct dialogue between the Obama administration and the American public." No such office had previously existed. It oversees the official White House website, which is managed by former high-level staffers from Obama's media team and which was designed, like the campaign website, by Blue State Digital.

Through this process, Obama has taken to becoming the first YouTube president, reading the presidential weekly radio address online as well as over the airwaves.

He's provided Americans with an interactive way to track legislation, ask questions of him, and follow the progress of the White House agenda. Unlike any president before him, Barack Obama is commander-in-chief of the digital age.

Now there are plenty of people who see the accomplishments of the Obama campaign as impressive, but see the long-term impact of the operation as minimal. After all, every metric used to measure the success of the organization centers around the candidate himself. The operation was perfectly built and masterfully executed, but it was a once-in-a-generation politician who powered its success. Given that, the likelihood that another Democrat will be able to replicate that kind of excitement is unlikely. Obama was the right candidate at the right moment.

That assessment is partially right. It's unlikely that Obama's successor—or any of the future Democratic nominees to follow—will capture the national mood so perfectly and inspire millions with such a seeming ease. But while counterintuitive, that actually presents a bigger crisis for Republicans than for Democrats.

The Obama list is now owned by the Democratic National Committee. It's a part of the Democratic infrastructure. And over the next four years, Organizing for America and other arms of the Democratic Party will continue to develop and update that list, keeping it fresh and comprehensive. That list will become the starting point of Obama's reelection and of his successor's election thereafter. The kind of top-of-the-line organization needed to compete has already been put together.

The Obama campaign couldn't have built it that way without a candidate as inspiring as Obama. So, for the GOP to compete—for it to build the kind of organization that can match Obama's—it will need its own Obama-like figure, someone who can inspire the Republican Party like no candidate has since Ronald Reagan. Anything short of that, even if accompanied by a new media operation as sophisticated as Obama's, will fail to produce the kind of infrastructure the Democrats will be starting with.

What's worse for the GOP is that, even if it does find the next Reagan—even if it finds such a person sometime in the next few election cycles—Republicans will find themselves playing catch-up. As of the 2008 campaign, the Democratic Party has a four-year head start. Its organization is fully built, ready to compete, and constantly being improved upon.

While in the off-season, as the GOP is trying to rebuild its own organization, the new media strategists in the Democratic Party are figuring out how to make substantial improvements to their already-groundbreaking operation.

For example, as sophisticated and integrated as the Obama new media operation was, certain parts of it lacked the kind of integration that could only be developed over a longer period of time. Take the field program, for example. Almost every Democratic campaign in the country uses software called the Voter Activation Network (known as the VAN) to provide it with voter contact information. This software provides access to a database of registered voters in the area that can be sorted into categories such as party affiliation, voting habits, location, age, race, and religion. When a volunteer from a campaign comes knocking on your door, it's usually because you fit criteria for the type of voter that campaign was looking to target. That's how your name ended up on the list that volunteer has clipped to her clipboard.

It was a critical trove of data for the Obama campaign, as it would be for any campaign, but it wasn't part of the campaign's online tools. According to the Wilburforce report, the VAN "was never successfully integrated with the Blue State Digital tools that managed the online organizing program, much to the dismay of many involved in the campaign." The reason was primarily a lack of time—time that the Organizing for America team has plenty of now.

That's another way the GOP finds itself at a real disadvantage. While Republicans are frantically scrambling to match the technological advances of the Obama operation, Democrats are building an even more sophisticated operation. While Democratic techies are focusing on improving the functionality of things like social networking and emerging text messaging technology, they will continue to place the Democratic infrastructure capability on an entirely different level than the GOP.

The GOP will have to outpace the Democratic Party to catch up, outpace it at a time when the Democratic Party has a comparative monopoly on new media talent and technical expertise. Until the GOP can parody the Democrats' Internet-driven success, and unless it finds a once-in-a-generation candidate of its own, the Democrats will hold a long-term, one-sided structural advantage over the only other major party in the country.

The Obama campaign didn't just build an organization that could win a single election; it built one that could sustain a permanent majority. The lasting infrastructure left behind in critical states and on the Internet will continue to grow over time—especially during Obama's re-election. The crippled Republican Party will face enormous challenges as it attempts to build a similar capacity—even more so when it comes to identifying a national candidate who can inspire the country in the way Obama did.

For the Republican Party, that's a pretty substantial problem. Those kinds of candidates come along every generation or so, and in this political climate, the only kind who could emerge and mobilize the right would be someone whose politics were aligned with the Tea Party— someone who would face impossible challenges on the general election stage.

By the time the 2012 election rolls around, the Republican Party might finally understand, from an organizational perspective, just how much trouble it's really in.

FIVE

☆ ☆ ☆

Obama 2012

We're getting killed. We're going to get killed. We're going to get our asses kicked.
  —*Howard Wolfson, Hillary Clinton's campaign communications director, shortly before the results of the Iowa caucus were announced*

For the Democrats to secure a permanent majority, Barack Obama is going to have to win reelection. The good news for Democrats is that, even at this early juncture, Barack Obama is poised to almost surely win that race. Of course, there are hundreds of news cycles between now and then, just as many policy decisions to be made, and potential for all sorts of unforeseeable events to occur. But the mechanics of what will come in 2012 help ensure that only in the rarest of circumstances will it be possible for Obama to lose reelection. In fact, short of a massively damaging scandal, something so dramatic it might cause him to resign the presidency, Barack Obama is going to win a second term in office. Here's how:

As I discussed in the last chapter, Obama will be starting the 2012 campaign where he left off in 2008. That means that the day he announces that he will seek reelection, instead of having to start from scratch, he'll have a 13 million person database to mobilize. In his first months of fundraising, he should be able to raise money at nearly the same rate as he had been at the end of the 2008 campaign. That means that instead of shocking the country with a $25 million total after the first three months, Barack Obama may well be on his way to the $300 million mark by that same time.

The 2012 campaign will almost surely raise well over a billion dollars, dwarfing the operations of his challengers and the 2008 operation that put him in the White House. The campaign will have enough money to advertise with a budget on par with some of the top corporations in the country. And without a serious primary to contend with, Barack Obama will be able to bank the money he raises in 2011, while his opponents are furiously spending the smaller amounts they're raising to beat one another.

With that kind of money, he'll be able to credibly expand the electoral map in two ways. First, he can invest in states like Georgia and Arizona, where losses in 2008 belied the potential that these states both have to turn blue. Georgia has a substantial minority population, with African Americans making up 30 percent of the 2008 electorate (98 percent of whom chose Obama). The surge in turnout there meant that Obama lost the state by only five points (compared to John Kerry's seventeen-point loss in the 2004 presidential election).

In Arizona, the 2008 contest might have gone differently had the Republican nominee not called the state home. With John McCain on the ballot, Arizona was the only southwestern state that the Obama campaign chose not to compete in. But Arizona has one of the highest populations of Hispanic voters in the country and has the potential to become a truly competitive state for Democrats. In their state-by-state guide to the 2008 election, NBC Political Director Chuck Todd and NBC Elections Director Sheldon Gawiser describe the state as Obama's number one new target for 2012, arguing that "an Obama-run Democratic Party will probably do whatever it takes to lay the groundwork for making Arizona a battleground state by 2012."

The second thing Obama can do to expand the Democrats' electoral map is to pursue investments in states where the purpose would primarily be to build party infrastructure for future campaigns. In those states, the Obama campaign won't pull off a victory, but its registration efforts could pay dividends down the line. In Texas, for example, a substantial investment by the Obama campaign could help the state turn blue an election cycle or two earlier than it otherwise would. The result wouldn't affect the 2012 race, but it could have a lasting effect on creating a Democratic permanent majority.

An expanded map and an unmatchable organization in size and scope will make Obama the most formidable incumbent in modern American history, making it impossible for any of his opponents to credibly go toe-to-toe.

That reality will not be lost on the GOP, as the field of potential candidates begins considering the possibility of challenging Obama for the White House.

At this stage, we can't know with certainty who will choose to run. But for the Republican Party, the question of who will run is less important than the question of who won't. With Obama's strength comes two problems for the GOP. The first is the sheer impossibility of competing against an organization the size of Obama's. The second is the fear of it.

There will be plenty of Republicans who won't take into consideration the uphill battle they will face. But among the few potential challengers with good heads on their shoulders—among those who haven't yet been blinded by the backward, anti-intellectual elements of their party—challenging Obama will seem like a fairly ill-advised career move. Running for president and losing hasn't destroyed every politician. Ronald Reagan and George H. W. Bush won the presidency after losing a previous attempt. Al Gore and Joe Biden got to be vice president. Hillary Clinton got to be secretary of state. But for most potential candidates, knowing that a loss is all but inevitable is sufficient to dissuade them from getting into the race.

Take Jon Huntsman, former governor of Utah, for example. Huntsman was a relatively moderate Republican governor in one of the most conservative states, where he enjoyed approval ratings above 80 percent. He maintained those approval ratings even after publicly supporting civil unions, a markedly progressive position for such a conservative state. In April 2009, Obama campaign manager David Plouffe unintentionally elevated Huntsman onto the national stage by suggesting that he was one of the few Republican politicians who appeared formidable in 2012.

And understandably so. Huntsman is young, amiable, and exceptionally articulate. When he speaks, he exudes reasonableness. While Republican governors like Bobby Jindal and Mark Sanford were rejecting stimulus money for their states in 2009, withholding essential services from their poorest constituencies to boost their conservative credentials, Huntsman went on MSNBC in February 2009 and called his fellow Republicans out, describing their actions as "gratuitous political griping."

He has the potential to be for the Republican Party what Obama was for the Democrats in 2008—a man capable of simultaneously exciting his base while appealing to an ever-more critical group of Independent voters. To hear him speak is to know he's a Republican an Independent would love.

But Huntsman didn't take the bait. Likely sensing the impossible nature of a race against Obama, he chose to join the administration instead, becoming the U.S. ambassador to China. Doing so took him entirely off the stage (a wise move by the Obama team), but it also provided him with a valuable addition to his résumé should he decide to seek the presidency sometime after 2012.

There's also Florida governor Charlie Crist. Crist was

one of the most popular governors in the country, and Florida is one of the most critical battleground states. For most politicians, those two facts would be sufficient to seriously consider a run. But, like Huntsman, Crist recognized that going up against the Obama political machine would be a Hail Mary pass in the dark. He had enough political sense to understand that a race against Obama would likely be unwinnable. Though he easily could have left the governor's mansion to concentrate fully on building his national profile and running for president, Crist decided to run for a Senate seat instead (a move, albeit, that proved equally treacherous).

The refusal of strong GOP politicians to consider running in the 2012 presidential election is a crushing reality for the Republican Party and perhaps the single most compelling reason that Obama will be reelected. If you're talented enough to be president one day, you're also smart enough not to try in 2012.

That, of course, brings us to the next reason that Barack Obama is going to win his reelection: the Republican nominee.

With top-tier contenders shying away from the contest, those who are left to run will be a highly dysfunctional group. There will be the likes of Newt Gingrich and Bobby Jindal, who may be convinced to run just by hearing themselves mentioned on cable news as potential candidates. There will be those who will run purely to further a single issue, without expectation of winning a contest. Tom Tancredo, the champion of anti-immigrant sentiment, comes to mind. There will, of course, be those who run this time because they didn't make it last time, those whose name identification still remains high enough for them to score well in early polling. Mike Huckabee, who won the Value Voters Summit Straw Poll in September 2009, may end up among that category. So might Mitt Romney, who many see as the early frontrunner in the race.

But whether they sign up to run out of ego or ambition or media anointment, whether they expect to win or are just trying to broaden their profile, those who join the race will embark on a year-long primary campaign, undergoing a process that will almost assuredly produce a nominee from the right-most flank of the party.

Here's why:

Republican primary voters are extremely conservative. To court their votes, candidates need to come with certain credentials that appeal to evangelicals and working-class white men. To build their campaigns, they need to excite the activist base of the party, both to raise money and to recruit volunteers. For a candidate who lacks the ability to mobilize the base, securing the Republican nomination will be almost impossible.

So, for a full year, as candidates vying for that nomination present their credentials and spar with one another, the candidates who move furthest and fastest to the right are those most likely to benefit. By the time January 2012 rolls around, the only serious candidates still standing will face off in the Iowa caucus and New Hampshire primary, two contests that are sure to define the rest of the race.

Since 1976, Iowa has held the first caucus and New Hampshire the first primary during every presidential primary season. It's a tradition that infuriates senators and governors of other states, but one unlikely to change anytime soon. By coming first, these contests tend to shape public opinion dramatically. After a year of campaigning and predictions, they are the first tangible hints of results.

That makes them enormous media stories, even among those who had previously been unengaged in the primary process. When Barack Obama won the Iowa caucus, the news was the top headline of every political website that night and every newspaper in the country the next morning. It consumed the news cycle for days, driven entirely by the positive coverage of Obama as a winner. The conversation about the race completely changed. It was no longer about Hillary Clinton and an approaching inevitability. Suddenly it was about a head-to-head race with two of the most impressive politicians the Democratic Party had seen in a long time. Obama's poll numbers went up dramatically in just about every state, helping position him to secure the nomination.

That's what the campaign had been banking on. It's why campaign staff had focused so relentlessly on Iowa. Temo Figueroa, Obama's national field director, described a win in Iowa as the equivalent of spending over $100 million in paid ads. That's how big an impact a victory there can have and why the early states are so important to campaigns and the journalists who cover them.

When the Republican candidates get to Iowa, the depth

of the party's impending troubles will be obvious. In 2008, 60 percent of Republican caucus-goers in Iowa were evangelicals. Ninety-nine percent were white. Eighty-eight percent called themselves conservative. It's about as right-wing a group of voters as assembles anywhere in the country. The winner of that contest will become one of only two viable candidates for the nomination. The other will be the winner of the New Hampshire primary.

Unlike Iowa, New Hampshire's primary electorate is not dominated by evangelicals. Republican primary voters in New Hampshire are still quite conservative, but they tend to present a characteristically libertarian streak. Also unlike Iowa, New Hampshire holds an open primary. That means that unaffiliated Independent voters can choose to vote in either primary and can make that decision on the day of the election without changing party registration. In 2008, one of the biggest stories leading up to the New Hampshire primary was how many Independents would choose the Democratic ballot and how many would grab the Republican one.

But in 2012, there will be no Democratic primary to speak of. There will be a Democratic ballot, and President Obama's name will be on it, but he will almost surely be running unopposed. During the long primary season, all the action will be on the Republican side, and Independents who show up to vote in January will likely heavily favor the Republican ballot.

The result: New Hampshire, which already has a comparatively moderate GOP primary electorate, will see that electorate move further to the left. That means that New Hampshire will almost certainly vote for a different candidate than the winner of the Iowa caucus. In fact, in the more than thirty years since both states held the first nominating contests, no nonincumbent Republican has ever won both states. In that same period, no Republican has ever secured the nomination without winning at least one. Never. Not once. Not ever.

After Iowa and New Hampshire, the race will take its clearest shape. The more conservative candidate—and winner of the Iowa caucus—will find himself or herself in a showdown with a more-moderate candidate, the winner of New Hampshire. Next up: South Carolina.

South Carolina's Republican primary voters are generally just as conservative as those in Iowa. In 2008, like in Iowa, 60 percent were evangelicals and more than 95 percent were white. This tends to allow the more conservative candidate (usually the winner of the Iowa caucus) to defeat the more moderate choice (usually the winner in New Hampshire). In 2000, for example, after then-Governor Bush defeated John McCain in Iowa, McCain bounced back with an impressive victory in New Hampshire, propelled by a voting population skeptical of Bush's ideological conservatism. But the next contest was in South Carolina, where voters shared more in common ideologically with Iowa's voters than New Hampshire's. Bush's win there gave him the momentum to secure the nomination.

Winning South Carolina is critical. The last of the early states, it is the final battlefield before Super Tuesday. For both parties, that makes South Carolina important, but it's especially critical for the GOP. Unlike the Democratic Party, many Republican primary contests have winner-take-all rules. The winner of the race takes all of the delegates of that state rather than just a proportion based on his or her win. With that formulation, the frontrunner on Super Tuesday is usually able to stack up enough delegates on that single day to unofficially secure the nomination. It's why John McCain's nomination fight was over long before Barack Obama defeated Hillary Clinton. For the GOP, Super Tuesday becomes the whole ball game.

The most likely scenario, then, is that the winner of the Iowa caucus will go on to win South Carolina and will use the momentum of that victory to secure the nomination on Super Tuesday. In fact, since 1980, every winner of the South Carolina primary has gone on to become the Republican nominee.

But while it is indeed most likely, we know from recent history that this isn't the only possible scenario. It's also possible to have a scenario play out in 2012 like the one that did for John McCain in 2008.

McCain was never the darling of the base. He had once called Jerry Falwell and those on the religious right "agents of intolerance." He bucked his party in the Senate often and carried the maverick label with pride. He was a favorite Republican among Democrats, much in the way that Joe Lieberman was a favorite Democrat among Republicans. Still, in 2008, he grabbed the Republican nomination.

It required a true confluence of events. Without the support of the activist base, the McCain campaign spent most of 2007 as a dark-horse candidacy. It was almost always out of money. By December 2007, John McCain had already received a $3 million bank loan to finance his floundering campaign, which he collateralized by taking out a life insurance policy. When he returned to the bank for another $1 million, he had to secure that loan with a pledge to accept federal matching funds and to stay in the race long enough to receive them.

But the campaign didn't collapse, as it should have, largely because of events that unfolded in Iowa, beyond McCain's control. Mitt Romney had spent most of 2007 with a healthy lead in the Iowa caucus. A relatively moderate former Massachusetts governor, Romney had courted the far-right voters of the Iowa caucus by dramatically shifting his positions to match theirs. When he was governor, he was pro-choice and pro-gun-control and even once said something bad about Ronald Reagan on television. But in Iowa, he was pro-life, pro-gun, anti-gay, and anti-immigrant.

Yet, as caucus day approached, Iowa voters developed doubts, slowly starting to see through the Romney facade. Romney's shifting positions were contradictory, and they seemed that way to voters. Among evangelicals, his Mormonism was a prime reason they distrusted him. And so, in an enormous upset, despite spending more money than any other candidate in the state, Mitt Romney was beaten by Mike Huckabee, who, at the time, had only fourteen staffers on his entire campaign.

The win was unprecedented. During an election season in which the big news story was the importance of campaign organization, Mike Huckabee had taken the Iowa caucus with a tiny group of staffers led by his daughter. The loss was, more or less, the end of Romney's candidacy and the event most responsible for John McCain becoming the nominee. Had Romney not been so remarkably unappealing to Iowa voters, he probably would have secured the nomination for himself. Instead, Huckabee became the guy to beat. He would surely be the one to go head to head with whomever was about to win the New Hampshire primary, settling once and for all who would be the Republican nominee.

But while Huckabee's win in Iowa gave him a helpful boost in upcoming contests, his total lack of campaign infrastructure made it impossible for him to capitalize on the positive coverage. He didn't have enough field staff to recruit volunteers, not enough volunteers to identify supporters, and not enough financial support to come anywhere close to knocking off McCain's candidacy.

With no real momentum to speak of, Huckabee settled into second place. McCain won a come-from-behind victory in New Hampshire, then beat Huckabee in South Carolina, fueling his ride all the way to the nomination.

It was an incredibly unlikely occurrence, requiring a highly unusual set of circumstances. If the winner of the Iowa caucus had been running a full-scale campaign, it never would have happened. It almost surely won't happen again in 2012.

But even if it does, let's not forget what John McCain had to become in order to secure that nomination. He may have begun the campaign as a moderate, but by the end, he had to tack so far to the right that Barack Obama was able to defeat him by accurately painting him as a character from the wingnut crowd, completely in step with George W. Bush. A moderate won't ever secure the Republican nomination without giving up on moderation. The way the system is set up simply will not allow it. McCain's candidacy was certainly proof of that.

We can be confident, then, that the Republican nominee will be either a friend of the activist base or someone who is trying really hard to become one. And when that winner emerges on the general election stage, no longer focused exclusively on impressing the primary electorate, he or she will be straddled with untenable positions—totally divorced from the mainstream—making the challenge of winning a national election almost entirely insurmountable.

Let's recap for a minute. Obama will have an organization that will be unmatchable in size and strength. He'll be able to break all his previous fundraising records. And he'll be going up against a second-tier right-wing candidate whose views will surely contradict those of the majority of Americans. That alone sounds like a recipe for an Obama victory. But there's more:

Between 2008 and 2012, the political landscape will have gotten better for Democrats, not worse. Between 2 and 4 million immigrants will have been naturalized and registered to vote. Another 16 million young people will have become eligible voters. The population growth in metropolitan and suburban areas, places where Obama did especially well in 2008, will continue to surge.

The Republican Party will also find itself dealing with a fading battleground. As Todd and Gawiser describe in their analysis, there are seven states that are on the verge of losing their status as key battlegrounds in presidential elections.

"Some have become more Democratic because of changes in demographics," they explain. Among those are states like Nevada, which is the country's fastest-growing state. Most of that population growth has occurred in and around Las Vegas, which is the Democrats' strongest-performing region statewide. Major growth in Hispanic turnout also played a large role in Obama's 2008 victory there. It was the same story in New Mexico, where Hispanic growth helped propel Obama to a fifteen-point win.

"Others," they add, "have become less of a battleground due to economic conditions." Among those are Pennsylvania and Michigan, both electoral-vote-rich states that Republicans love to compete in. But even at the height of GOP dominance, neither has shown any sign of flipping to the Republican Party. A Republican nominee hasn't won either state in over twenty years.

In total, the seven states Todd and Gawiser identify— Michigan, Minnesota, Nevada, New Hampshire, New Mexico, Pennsylvania, and Wisconsin—represent a total of seventy-two electoral votes that will no longer be available to a diminishing Republican Party. That will make the road back to 270—the number of electoral votes needed for victory—that much more rocky for the GOP.

And so when Obama enters the 2012 contest, he will do so with an organization that will be competing against an out-of-touch opponent and in a political environment that will make it significantly easier for his campaign to win 270 electoral votes and secure the White House for another four years. That sounds pretty good. But if you're still not convinced, know that Obama also has history on his side.

Indeed, history does tell a similar story. Obama was not the first man elected president in a landslide while the opposition party was in power. But if he lost reelection, that would indeed be a first. Since the founding of the country, no president has ever been elected under such circumstances and then lost reelection. It's never happened. What's more is that, since the nineteenth century, the only time a party lost control of the White House after holding it for only four years was after Jimmy Carter's defeat in 1980. For Obama to lose reelection he would need to be, from a historical perspective, a groundbreaking failure.

And even then—even if he were to become Carter reborn sometime around his third year in office—he'd still be going up against a Republican Party devoid of ideas and plans, one that has failed entirely to provide reasonable alternatives to the progressive agenda. Obama will be facing an opposition party still largely controlled by the fringe. Even if the economy is still in crisis, it's hard to imagine the American people turning their back on a president, who by then will be able to tout legitimate progress, in exchange for a party incapable of serious conversation. Franklin Roosevelt got elected again and again during the Great Depression not because he cured the economy, but because voters trusted that he was working hard at it, they saw tangible results, and they understood that the Republican alternative was consistently unacceptable.

"No amount of misrepresentation or statistical contortion can conceal or blur or smear [my] record," said FDR on the eve of the 1936 election. "Neither the attacks of unscrupulous enemies nor the exaggerations of over-zealous friends will serve to mislead the American people."

That's what should give you great confidence about Obama's chances in 2012. It's not just that he will have a superior organization (though he will) or that he's a once-in-a-generation politician (though he is). It's that he will be competing against a Republican Party that has marginalized itself to a point where it can no longer elect a president.

By the time the Republican nominee has emerged from the primaries, the perils of the general election will be crippling, leaving him or her truly incapable of competing. And the territory will be challenging. In 2008, Obama won 365 electoral votes. He could have won without California and New York, or without Florida, without Ohio, without a chunk of the Northeast. He won states like Indiana, Virginia, and North Carolina, which hadn't voted for a Democrat in forty-four years. This was a landslide in its truest form. A winning Republican in 2012 would have to wrestle ninety-six electoral votes from the president to defeat him. Even in the best of conditions, that's an overwhelmingly difficult task.

Policy matters. If the economy is still in shambles when Obama runs for reelection, it will make the campaign more difficult. If he fails to pass key pieces of his agenda or continues to be perceived as having let deficits spiral out of control, he will no doubt face some moderate backlash. But the mechanical realities—the sheer disparity in parties from organization and infrastructure to the quality of the candidates—are immensely one-sided. It's not that Obama can't lose under any circumstances. It's that, given the way the Republican narrative has unfolded, given the way that we know Obama can build a campaign operation, given the volume of investments Obama will be able to make to spread out the electoral map, defeating him will require a set of circumstances that simply will not exist in 2012.

Of course, the media won't portray the race that way. Covering a presidential campaign is like main-lining heroin for most political reporters, whether on cable news, in print, or in the blogosphere. But in order to keep the conversation going twenty-four hours a day for twelve months before the first contest, media outlets tend to produce and rely on data that they know, or at least should know, reflecting very little accuracy about the outcome of the race. The most common such example is sure to be their constant obsession with meaningless national polls. We can expect countless analysts making predictions about the race based on entirely irrelevant data.

The problem, of course, is that national polling tells us very little, if anything, about the state of a primary race. It's the state-by-state victories in Iowa, New Hampshire, and beyond that determine the outcome of the race, not the general national mood as described by polls conducted many months prior. Especially during the primaries, national polls will provide little more than a topic of conversation for pundits to chew on when there isn't much else to pontificate about.

Here's what we do know: It is often the case that the leader in an early national poll goes on to lose the race shortly after the first nominating contests begin. The 2008 campaign provides perfect examples of this. As late as September 2007, Chris Matthews was using national polling to predict that the battle for the presidency would almost certainly come down to Hillary Clinton versus Rudy Giuliani. Hillary Clinton had held a double-digit lead over Barack Obama in almost every national poll taken during the first nine months of 2007. Giuliani's name recognition—his self-branding as 9/11 hero also propelled him to sizable national leads over his Republican opponents during the same period.

It didn't matter to most journalists that Hillary Clinton was struggling in Iowa. It didn't matter to most journalists that Rudy Giuliani had given up competing in the early primary states. That the national polls pegged these two as the leaders was all the chattering class needed to define them the same way.

It's not that members of the media don't know any better. Early polls showed Joe Lieberman beating John Kerry in 2004. In 1991, national polls put Bill Clinton in last place, more than twenty-five points behind the leader. Their inaccuracy is consistent and well documented; these are lessons that have long been learned. But the media has a vested interest in original content to fill the twenty-four-hour cycle. And so, on cable and network news, during the Sunday talk shows, and throughout the blogosphere, the race is sure to be defined using data that isn't particularly relevant to its ultimate outcome.

It will also be in the interest of journalists to describe Obama's reelection not as a foregone conclusion, but as a head-to-head battle that could go either way. A race that's anybody's game will always produce better ratings than a nearly guaranteed victory for the incumbent.

As long as you don't get caught up in that conversation, as long as you can keep your eye on the critical dynamics at play, you'll find the 2012 election to be far less stressful than 2008. Obama's organization will be unstoppable, his financial totals insurmountable, his opponent weak and out of touch, and the political landscape especially favorable for Democrats. To secure a permanent majority, Barack Obama will need to win reelection. In 2012, he'll do just that.

SIX

☆ ☆ ☆

Obama 2.0

*Don't speak ill of your predecessors or successors. You
didn't walk in their shoes.*

—*Donald Rumsfeld*

After 2012, if all has gone well, the Democrats will
have been in power in Congress for six years. The
most recent election will have been the first with the newly
redistricted map in the House of Representatives. Democrats will have picked up a dozen seats on that fact alone.
President Obama will have been reelected. His campaign
will have injected millions upon millions of dollars into
state organizations. His turnout operation will have
helped defend vulnerable congressional seats and helped
Democrats reclaim seats lost in 2010. It's the end of 2012
and the federal government is still very much a Democratic stronghold.

The Democratic majority in Congress will likely hold

through 2016, sustained by redistricting, reinforced by a strong progressive agenda, and nudged along with the help of a diminished Republican Party. Those demographic changes that helped create new Democratic seats will also swell the ranks of Democratic voters in critical states. At-risk seats—and states—will steadily become less vulnerable. Save for a few major Democratic scandals in a row, the party should continue to maintain majority control.

But in 2016, the hopes of a Democratic permanent majority will be challenged more seriously than at any previous moment. Though scores of progressives will wish otherwise, Barack Obama will be unable to seek a third term as president (a pesky little thing known as the Twenty-second Amendment). By 2016, Democrats will need to find someone to replace him.

Historically speaking, that's not an easy task. Since term limits on the presidency were ratified in 1947, the White House has been held by a single party for more than eight years only one time. Ronald Reagan served eight years and George H. W. Bush served the four that followed. At no other time during the modern presidency has a party finished eight years in office and then convinced the American people to let them have at it again. It's simply one of the toughest things to pull off in American politics. (And if you're going to try, running against Michael Dukakis helps tremendously.)

The election of 2016 represents the single-greatest challenge for the twenty-first-century Democratic Party.

It will be a moment of truth—a chance for the party to prove that its success need not be tied exclusively to Barack Obama, that there is promise for the party, a clear direction and vision, beyond the Obama horizon. By the beginning of his second term, President Obama needs to begin preparing the party for his successor.

Leadership has to be about more than dependency. There is a quality about Obama that his strongest supporters fawn over—a calmness that says, "Don't worry, I'll take care of it. I'll get it done. I got this." Obama has an ego befitting his job title and a confidence that he can handle whatever comes his way. After his first debate with John McCain, he received an e-mail from his political director, Patrick Gaspard: "You are more clutch than Michael Jordan," it read. "Just give me the ball," Obama quipped back.

Thus far, in large part, that's what the country has done. We gave him the ball. And he's delivered. But at some point, Obama will have to be clear that these issues do not require him and him alone. He'll have to prepare the party to confront the challenges ahead within the framework of his political vision. But, in doing so, he must, for the sake of a long-term progressive agenda, set the party and the country on a path to accomplish it without him. This is, perhaps, the single-greatest challenge of good leadership—placing the vision ahead of the visionary.

The election of 2016 is critical. Finding a worthy successor to Obama, someone with the political talents and wisdom to take up his mantle, will be the difference between repeating the same basic pattern of history—one in which the success of parties ebbs and flows—versus writing an entirely new chapter in which Democrats rule the next political era.

In all likelihood, Joe Biden won't be a factor. Though he hasn't yet ruled out running for president in 2016, Joe Biden will turn seventy-five years old several weeks after that election day. That would make him the oldest person to assume the presidency in U.S. history, a distinction that would likely prevent his election and dissuade him from even seeking it. But even if Joe Biden were a rising star in the party, it would be better for the party if he didn't run.

It's better for a president not to have a vice president who's looking for a promotion—someone without a separate political and personal ambition. And it helps the party in that it prevents a president from hand-selecting a successor eight years ahead of schedule. When the vice president runs, it is with the institutional support of the party. The nomination is almost always guaranteed.

In 2008, when the Republican Party was soul searching, trying to determine how and with whom it would replace George W. Bush, the person whose opinion seemed least relevant was Bush's. It wasn't his party anymore. It wasn't his future Republicans were envisioning; it was their own. Had Bush chosen a younger, more likable, and more politically inclined vice president, there would not have been a fight for the Republican nomination—at least not in the way it actually unfolded. Bush's vice president, had he run, would have been the party's frontrunner by default. All the institutional support available would have been behind him. Other potential candidates would have been strong-armed into backing off. Replacing Bush would have been left to party insiders, not the party at large.

That's what happened in 2000 for the Democrats. For all the well-deserved accolades that Al Gore has received in his postpolitical life, and perhaps, in part, because of them, average observers seem to have largely forgotten how inept a candidate Gore actually was. He was stiff, unconnected, unconnectable. His answers to questions were formulaic and distant. He was seen as arrogant and condescending. And, while there isn't much doubt that Gore actually won the 2000 presidential election, it's also perfectly clear that a stronger candidate would have made it all the way to the White House.

Gore would not have been the natural choice of the people. But he was Bill Clinton's choice, eight years earlier. And so the party stood with him, even when he struggled in Iowa, even when progressives balked. That, more than anything, is how George Bush became president.

Even if Biden were younger, he'd be the wrong pick by default. Obama shouldn't get to choose his own successor, especially not eight years in advance. That's a decision for Democratic voters.

Still, Obama must play a role in making sure that his supporters, his volunteers, and his donors—the whole of the newly made Democratic establishment—participate in the 2016 primaries in the same way they did in 2008. Obama has to encourage the transfer of his organization to the rest of the party. He shouldn't do that by endorsing a candidate, but by encouraging his supporters to choose a campaign and by giving them a way of thinking about that choice. Obama can inspire those who made such strong commitments to his candidacy to make a similar commitment to a candidate of their choosing based on a standard that's good for them and the future of the party.

In doing so, Obama can help prove that the infrastructure he helped build for the party can be permanent and transferable.

So how are we going to do it? To a large degree, it will be up to us to seek out the right candidate—the right *kind* of candidate. In the shadow of Obama, the inclination will be to try to find someone just like him—someone who can do it exactly as he does, who can replicate that kind of energy and that kind of excitement. On that front, we're likely to be profoundly disappointed. Barack Obama is a once-in-a-generation politician. His talent, his style, his gravitas, and his intellect all combine to inspire, in part, because such a combination is so rare. Obama is a man as big as the moment he was required to meet. He is a singular figure at a singular time. Had his rise to the national stage happened in a different year or had the depths of the nation's crisis and the unrelenting desire for change been something less, he may never have ascended to the presidency. We can't expect, and certainly can't hang our hopes on, events conspiring yet again to produce a story worthy of a masterful work of fiction.

But while Obama cannot be replicated, his playbook can—again and again. One of the broader narratives of the Obama versus Clinton primary fight in 2008 was how different Obama's political playbook was from Clinton's. Hers was essentially her husband's, a philosophy based on how politics worked in the 1980s and 1990s. It's not that President Clinton's playbook was bad. It got him elected president twice at a time when the Democratic Party was an unpopular brand. But it was different.

And in 2008, Obama's playbook was better.

It isn't an accident that Obama is perceived as honest, trustworthy, smart, and capable. It isn't a fluke that his answers to questions are clear and concise, that you rarely get the sense that he's ducking and dodging. It's not because he's a better person. It's because he understands good politics.

Barack Obama approached national politics with a few basic guiding principles. Voters aren't stupid. Voters don't like to be lied to. And voters want to see themselves in their president.

As mind-numbingly simple as that sounds, it isn't the mission statement of every political playbook. Among Democrats, it's often not even a consideration. Time and again, Democrats lost the presidency not because their ideas were worse or because the country was in a distinctly Republican mood, but because they failed to connect with voters.

Voters know what political phoniness sounds like. It's been one of the defining fixtures in American politics. Voters are, by now, veritable experts. And yet, phoniness is what the Democratic Party offered up again and again. When in March of 1999, for example, Al Gore was asked by CNN's Wolf Blitzer why he was running for president, he actually said this:

> Well, Wolf, I haven't formally announced my candidacy yet, but when I do, I will lay out a vision of what I want to see in this country in the twenty-first century. And the campaign won't be about me, it'll be about the American people, and I hope they'll choose that vision of a nation with strong families and livable communities, in harmony with all of our diversity and fully prepared to lead the world.

It's hard to know what that even means.

In October 2004, at the final presidential debate, when John Kerry was asked by Bob Schieffer if we had come far enough along that we could end affirmative action, these were the first hundred words of his response:

> No, Bob, regrettably, we have not moved far enough along. And I regret to say that this administration has even blocked steps that could help us move further

along. I'll give you an example. I served on the Small Business Committee for a long time. I was chairman of it once. Now I'm the senior Democrat on it. We used to—you know, we have a goal there for minority set-aside programs, to try to encourage ownership in the country. They don't reach those goals. They don't even fight to reach those goals. They've tried to undo them.

You shouldn't have to be a senator to understand one. If our nominee talks like this in 2016, that's game over. No permanent majority. The cycle of history will continue. Eight years and out.

Obama understood this in 2008. So, rather than obfuscating and hedging, rather than trying hard to say nothing that will offend and nothing that will stir so that nothing is ever really said, Obama's answers were clear, his message crisp, his purpose understood.

In part, it may be that Obama, unlike many other Democrats, didn't fear the opposition. For years and years, Democrats, especially those in Congress, have operated under the assumption that Republican attacks against them are universally devastating and that unknown but catastrophic political consequences are always lurking somewhere just beyond the shadows.

Take Tom Daschle, former Senate minority leader and a close ally of the president. Obama had nominated Daschle to be secretary of Health and Human Services, a position that would have made him a point man on health care reform. When it was revealed during confirmation hearings that Daschle owed back taxes, Obama asked Daschle to hang tight and put up with a rockier confirmation hearing. Democratic Senators had already met privately with Daschle and had assured him that his nomination would not be derailed.

Still, later that week, when he picked up the *New York Times* and read an editorial calling for him to step down, Daschle called the president. He had concluded that he would be a distraction to the cause of health care reform if he continued with his fight, and he asked the president to accept his withdrawal.

A distraction to the cause of health care reform? For a man who spent nearly twenty years in the Senate, it was a surprisingly misguided bit of political reasoning. It's inconceivable that Daschle's rocky entrance into the Obama cabinet would have impacted his ability to get the job done with health care. There would have been plenty of stories about Daschle's taxes, to be sure, but those stories would have played out in full by February, a full four months before health care legislation would begin to move through Congress. Daschle's tax problems would never have been rehashed. He should have known this. But somehow, he didn't. And neither do many Democrats.

Obama's philosophy is a lot more reasonable. It recognizes that in the chaos of the twenty-four-hour news cycle, any given hour, any given news cycle is relatively meaningless. Unlike Daschle, Obama is able to take the long view. Where Daschle assumes that the short-term impact of a bad news story is the same as its long-term impact,

Obama knew all along that a political problem in February is ancient history four months and more than a hundred news cycles later.

There are some Democrats who act conservatively out of fear of being called liberal. There are others who understand they'll be called liberal regardless of how they act. Obama's replacement needs to come from the latter category—from among those who understand that the message of their own campaign is more important to shape than the message of their opponents'.

It'll be our job to find the right candidate and ours to reward those who exhibit critical qualities. And it's not just about how the candidate talks—it's about what they say. We'll need a politician who, when facing opposition to a progressive viewpoint, will reshape the argument rather than the position. In Obama's first major address to Congress, for example, he framed an unabashedly progressive agenda in terms of the country's economic well-being. Where President Clinton became famous for taking Republican ideas and wrapping them in Democratic arguments, President Obama called for some of the most liberal policies in a generation, and he did so using a fiscally conservative rationale.

Politicians who trust that their ideas are right are more likely to be able to persuade. They are better with their talking points and are able to add real depth. They sound more honest because they are more honest. Luckily, this ought to become less difficult for Democrats over time. As the population continues to become more progressive, voters are more likely to align with a progressive agenda anyway. But in the meantime, we need to avoid a nominee whose fear of his or her own beliefs will remind voters of John Kerry.

We need a candidate who can—who loves to—tell a story like Barack Obama. As legend goes, Obama hired the then-twenty-three-year-old Jon Favreau as a speechwriter in his Senate office in 2004 after asking Favreau what his speechwriting philosophy was. "I have no theory," offered Favreau, according to *Newsweek*. "But when I saw you at the [2004 Democratic national] convention, you basically told a story about your life from beginning to end, and it was a story that fit with the larger American narrative. People applauded not because you wrote an applause line but because you touched something in the party and the country that people had not touched before. Democrats haven't had that in a long time." Obama responded by offering Favreau the job.

Of all the stories that Obama told on the campaign trail, none was more important than his own. Voters want to see themselves in the president they elect. They want to understand their presidents' values, and they want to see a common thread. Bob Dole described choosing the president as less like picking a legislator and more like picking the person who will raise your kids if you die. It's about more than a set of policy prescriptions.

And so, throughout Obama's campaign, as he told the

unlikely story of his life, he made sure to emphasize the parts of it that were most relatable—parts of the broader American narrative. He understood what it meant to be poor because he was once. He understood the honor of military service because his grandfather was a hero in World War II. He understood what a hard day's work was all about because he worked for little money on the streets of Chicago. He understood what it meant to have faith. He understood hurt and suffering, hope and joy. In each of his speeches, he felt empathy.

He wasn't the first. It was Bill Clinton who mastered this talent. Of the things Clinton was always most proud of, being from "a placed called Hope" had to be at the top of the list. Even among those who aggressively opposed him, it was impossible for anyone, from working class to wealthy, to not see some of themselves in Bill Clinton's story.

Contrast that with Al Gore, who grew up in a hotel in Washington, D.C., while his father was a senator. That kind of life affords all sorts of opportunities, but the presidency shouldn't be one of them. A president should be uniquely gifted: a better manager than us, smarter than us, more capable than us. But he or she should still be one of us.

The candidate the Democrats choose in 2016 has to be able to tell his or her own story, stitched in a broader American context. It's not such an impossible task. Obama's story is beautifully interesting, but there are plenty of others that could measure up. And if Obama could so easily connect voters to an unlikely story, a lesser politician ought to be able to do the same thing with a likely one.

The candidate that Democrats rally behind doesn't have to be perfect from the beginning. Barack Obama says it took him four months to learn how to be a national candidate. He had plenty of subpar debate performances early on, and he was sometimes careless with his wording. But he learned quickly, and so too must his successor. In the minute-by-minute news cycle, all gaffes exist in an echo chamber. They are repeated and amplified, and if bad enough, they can define a candidacy.

Those mistakes are often not just the candidate's alone. Members of John Kerry's presidential team made the decision to have the senator photographed while windsurfing, even while fighting to make him appear more like an average American. It was Mark Penn, Hillary Clinton's chief strategist, who decided that "strength and experience" were a better message than "hope and change." It was Al Gore's advisers who cautioned that he not talk about the environment on the campaign trail and who kept Bill Clinton on the sidelines of that race. Campaigns can destroy great candidates. And candidates can destroy great campaigns. Success on a national stage requires a near-flawless candidate and a campaign staff that operates on a level equally high.

Perhaps most important of all, Democrats must unite behind a candidate with enough self-confidence to be willing to recalculate, to reformulate, and readjust. When things are going wrong, they need to be fixed. A candidate needs to be the chief executive of the campaign. It's an opportunity to demonstrate management style and sound decision making. When mistakes are made, candidates must ignore the old playbook, which requires they admit no wrong-doing, take no responsibility, shift blame, change the story, and change the subject. The American people can't stand someone who refuses to take responsibility. And we are suckers for a heartfelt apology.

After the Bay of Pigs invasion in 1961, President Kennedy held a news conference at which he took full responsibility for the fiasco. His job approval ratings went up. When Bill Clinton finally apologized for having lied about his affair with Monica Lewinsky, his job approval reached the midsixties. In his first few weeks in office, with tax problems emerging among a number of cabinet nominees, Obama took responsibility for not living up to the standard he'd set. "I consider this a mistake on my part, one that I intend to fix and correct and make sure that we're not screwing up again." Two-thirds of the public approved.

The old playbook is wrong. Taking responsibility for mistakes, as well as the steps to fix them, is a sign of strong leadership. And it's another way of being honest with the American people—a way for them to continue to build trust.

Finding a candidate who can do all of these things will not be easy; the stage isn't exactly glimmering with rising stars. But six years is a long time—full of opportunities for relative unknowns to jump onto the national scene. There are future governors who could be contenders who haven't been elected yet. Future senators, too. For now, the stage is mostly empty, save for the small possibility of Hillary Clinton. She would be sixty-nine years old on the day she took office, right on the border of what might be considered too old to run. And by then, she may be a figure who's drifted slowly off the stage.

But her candidacy is worth considering. Clinton took to her role as secretary of state much like she did as senator. She kept her head down, learned the job, mastered the job, and proved to everyone around her that she was worthy of the role. Part of that role has been to loyally serve the president, which she succeeded in doing from the very beginning. Her first public words upon nomination, and all those that have followed, have shown a genuine respect for the office of the president and a committed loyalty to Obama. On foreign policy issues, there is essentially no distance between the two on approach.

The divisions and frustrations that Clinton engendered among Obama supporters during the tumultuous primary fight have mostly evaporated. Democrats approve of her job performance at the State Department at a higher level than they approve of Obama's in the White House. If she were to run in 2016, she could do so, not as Obama's opposition, but as the heir to his legacy. She is a talented politician, surely capable of mastering Obama's political playbook, just as she mastered the last one. She can fill the role of a postpartisan candidate, a stateswoman whose time to lead has come.

Next to Obama, she's head and shoulders smarter than

any other person currently on the national stage. She's an incredibly talented politician. No doubt, had she hired David Axelrod and David Plouffe, and had Obama hired Mark Penn and Howard Wolfson, she would be president today. She has what it takes to win. And in the next eight years, she can continue to evolve, to become the kind of politician we should want to mass produce.

That doesn't mean she'll be the best choice. It's hard to know if she could ever represent the future instead of the past and if she can actually go through such a complete transformation. But her name will be mentioned, and most likely, she'll have to consider it. In July 2009 on *Meet the Press,* when asked about her future, she remarked, "I have absolutely no belief in my mind that that is going to happen, that I have any interest in it happening. You know, as I said, I, I am so focused on what I'm doing." It sounds like she's already considering it.

Beyond Clinton, there's the gang of senators who will consider running (and be considered) because they think they've patiently waited their turn. In John Kerry's case, every Democrat from his entering Senate class had already run for president, so it was his turn in 2004. Hillary waited out the 2004 election, thinking that 2008 would be her turn. Chris Dodd thought it was his turn in 2008, too. Joe Biden and Bill Richardson had similar thoughts.

Of course, the presidency isn't about taking turns or paying dues. It's about the right person for the moment. It's possible that the right person is, by coincidence or talent, a member of that gang of senators waiting to announce. But the odds have to be against it. The future of the party, the successor to the Obama legacy, is today, more likely than not, miles and miles away from that stage.

We just have to make sure to look.

Take Elizabeth Warren, for example. A Harvard professor who was tapped to be the chair of the congressional oversight panel overseeing the bank bailouts (the bailout watchdog), Warren has impressed just about everyone in Washington whom she has come in contact with. She's like Barack Obama in that way—a possessor of a keen ability to make people take notice. In her current position, she has taken on the role of advocate for the taxpayer and adversary to the banks. She has a populist streak, but she's measured and reasonable, on a seemingly honest quest for fairness and justice.

Politically, she is almost perfect. She has the raw talent and brains to take on CEOs and senators, and, despite a limited amount of time on a national stage, she is surprisingly well-polished in her interactions with the news media. Though she will be painted as an Ivy Leaguer, Warren was born in Oklahoma and attended college in Houston.

Between now and then, of course, she'll probably need a job promotion. It's hard to imagine a successful presidential campaign launched from the Consumer Financial Protection Agency. But given her exceptional rise thus far and the fondness she has earned for herself in Washington, it's difficult to imagine that a promotion isn't on the way in the next four to five years. Perhaps she'll be Obama's next treasury secretary. Or maybe she'll run for the Senate in 2012. Either way, people like Elizabeth Warren don't come around very often—she's definitely worth keeping an eye on.

Democratic voters don't always pick the right nominee. But in 2016, we have to. We have to be mindful of what it is we need from our president—which qualities actually matter. And we can't let the media make that decision for us. We have to set our own standard, find a candidate who can meet our own expectations, and then work as hard for that person as we did for Obama.

The standard matters. We need a nominee with raw political skill—someone who can navigate the chaos of a presidential campaign and come out on the other side largely the same. We need an intellectual giant—someone who has the capacity to chair a dozen meetings a day on the full gamut of issues and someone who has a deeply rational decision making style. We need a communicator who can connect with people in a genuine way, who can persuade people of the right position and move them to adapt to change. We don't need another Obama, but we should aim to come close.

When we find that person, and many of us will disagree about who he or she is, it will be up to us to transfer the massive Obama organization—the monolith that millions of Democrats were a part of—to the next in line. If the movement that Obama helped build dies with the end of his presidency, the agenda he advocated for, the agenda we advocated for, will be in serious jeopardy. In 2016, the future of the Democratic Party will be very much in our hands.

But it's not just about the presidency in 2016. The size and strength of the movement we build will determine whether the coattails of the nominee can keep Democrats in control in Congress. The landslide congressional victory of 2008 was as much a function of a national desire to reject Republican ideology as it was a function of the efficiency of the Obama field operation. In 2016, we'll need to repeat that effort.

It's also a critical year for our long-term goals and a turning point for the future of the Democratic Party. Success in 2016 will dramatically improve the chances for a full generation of Democratic rule. In the years that follow, other forces will be at play. Demographic changes will make the map so one-sidedly Democratic that winning the presidency will start getting easier and easier.

And changes in attitude—in how Americans see their world—will remake the political landscape, turning it into one where the most popular politicians are also the most progressive ones.

SEVEN

☆ ☆ ☆

The Times They Are A-Changin'

*History is cyclical, and it would be foolhardy to assume
that the culture wars will never return. But . . . in our
tough times, when any happy news can be counted as a
miracle, a 40-year exodus for these ayatollahs can pass
for an answer to America's prayers.*

—*Frank Rich*

In the 1960s and 1970s, the oldest of the baby boomers
were trying to reshape the world. Student activism on
college campuses was shining a spotlight on the Vietnam
War in a way the public had never experienced. Protests,
sit-ins, walk-outs; eighteen-, nineteen-, twenty-year-old
kids trying to change the direction of the country. In the
South, they marched for civil rights, joined the freedom
rides, volunteered for George McGovern's presidential
campaign. In the end, they had some success—Lyndon
Johnson buckled to the political pressure and chose not
to seek reelection. But over the long term, the baby boomers didn't achieve a lot of what they aimed for. True, they
had driven Johnson from power, but doing so resulted in

the Nixon presidency and the continuation of the Vietnam War. The events of the 1960s divided the generation and would continue to divide those coming of voting age. The same generation that tried to end the Vietnam War gave Ronald Reagan a landslide victory. Twice.

Bill Clinton was the first boomer president, but George W. Bush was the second, a mixed record that's particularly defining. Two generations later, the children of the boomers, the millennials, are poised to change the political landscape to a degree their parents were never able to achieve.

The millennial generation, those born between 1978 and 2000, is on the verge of taking control of American politics. Unlike the boomers, millennials are not divided. In fact, they are more liberal and more unified in their liberalism than any generation that has preceded them. And they are so significant in size that they actually outnumber the boomers.

Ruy Teixeira, the Democratic Party's demographics guru, compiled a sweeping study of the millennial generation for the Center for American Progress, which helps underscore just how valuable the millennial generation can be for building a permanent majority:

Millennials voted for Obama by a whopping thirty-four-point margin, 66 to 32 percent. They are unabashedly progressive: Almost 60 percent favor gay marriage. Eighty eight percent favored sweeping health care reform. They are more tolerant of racial differences than previous generations and are more likely to see women as equals. They support unions, believe government has an important role to play in society, and they don't mind paying taxes. Their viewpoints are in line with what Howard Dean described as the "Democratic wing of the Democratic party." And they are flooding the voting population.

On election day 2008, more young people showed up to vote than at any time in American history. But in 2008, about half of all millennials were too young to vote. According to Teixeira's report, in every year between now and 2018, 4 million new millennials will become eligible voters. By the time Obama's successor is running for re-election, a remarkable 40 percent of the eligible voters in the country will be from the millennial generation. Forty percent of all eligible voters! The idea of a permanent Democratic majority becomes a lot more plausible when you consider that extraordinary figure. The youngest generation, the most liberal generation ever, will dominate American politics.

Of course, it's possible that over the years, millennials will become more conservative. Those who have yet to enter the voting population might tilt the generation to the right when they finally do. And those who voted for Democrats may become disenchanted over time. But as polling expert Nate Silver noted on his website FiveThirty-Eight, history suggests such a dramatic turn is unlikely. Silver found that people tend to solidify their voting preferences at an early age and that the popularity of the president when a voter turns eighteen can best explain how they'll vote during their lifetime.

For example, among those who came of voting age during Bill Clinton's moderately popular Democratic presidency, there is a slightly higher-than-average number of self-described Democrats. Among those who came of voting age during the relatively popular Reagan years, there is a higher-than-average number of self-described Republicans. It works the other way, too. When a president is extremely unpopular, as with George W. Bush, the opposition party can swell. In this case, among those who came of voting age under Bush, Democrats hold a dramatic advantage.

If the same trend holds true for millennials, those who have already come of voting age under Bush will continue to be progressive voters as they age. And those who have yet to come of voting age will eventually do so largely under Barack Obama. If he can remain popular among young people over his eight years in office, he can help ensure that the entire millennial generation subscribes to a progressive outlook. In doing so, he can create a political atmosphere ripe for a Democratic permanent majority to take root.

Like Generation Xers, millennials have, at times, been criticized by those who came before them. But well before their prime, this generation has already made a permanent mark on politics and society. In the shadow of September 11, it was millennials who volunteered for duty in Afghanistan. When George Bush misled the country into invading Iraq, it was millennials who served two and three and four tours of duty and millennials who mobilized the country to oppose the war. When Barack Obama announced his candidacy, it was millennials who volunteered by the hundreds of thousands to organize tens of millions, and millennials who wrote his speeches. The founders of Facebook are millennials. So are the founders of YouTube. In a short time, millennials have already changed the direction of the country and the way we interact in it. They served in and stopped an unpopular war. They elected a president. And they are revolutionizing social networking in an upgraded digital age. Over time, their influence will only increase.

The landscape is shifting. The voting population is changing—dramatically. And it's not just that it's getting younger; it's getting more ethnic and more progressive. As that happens, the political landscape is becoming increasingly welcoming to progressive Democrats in every region of the country.

On no front has that been more critical than minority voting. In 2008, Barack Obama received 80 percent of the minority vote. That was driven, in part, by a huge surge of voting among black voters.

In the 1930s, black voters dramatically realigned with the Democratic Party. Before FDR, they had tended to vote Republican, especially in the South, where Democrats were responsible for Jim Crow laws and where the Republican Party was still associated with Abraham Lincoln. But when FDR swept into power in 1932, he did so by building a new coalition of Democratic voters, which included a large majority of black voters. Ever since, African

Americans have been the most loyal voting bloc of the Democratic Party.

In 2008, they voted in their largest numbers to date. Two million more turned out than had in 2004. In the past, African American turnout had lagged behind the rest of the population. But with the first black presidential nominee and because of a massive turnout effort concentrated on black voters, African Americans turned out at a higher rate than all other registered voters. And 95 percent voted for Barack Obama.

That difference helped shape the 2008 race in critical battleground states like North Carolina, Michigan, Ohio, and Indiana. High black turnout helped guarantee Barack Obama the presidency.

Still, there is an argument to be made that this increased turnout was driven so much by the race of the presidential nominee that, in a post-Obama world, black voters will return to more depressed turnout figures. But that misses a critical point about voting behavior. Ask any political strategist working on any serious campaign on either side of the aisle, and he or she will agree: The most explanatory variable about whether someone will vote in the next presidential election is whether he or she voted in the last one. Put another way, people who vote once tend to vote twice. A one-time voter is a relatively rare voter.

So, when someone does go to the polls, there's a good chance he or she will be a voter in the next election of its kind. It's how political operatives figure out who to target with every campaign and how pollsters figure out who to poll. It's not a universal rule or a guarantee, but it is the case that people who become engaged in the political process, irrespective of the reason, tend to stay engaged. It's why voter registration drives are such a powerful political tool. Their impact is felt for many election cycles to follow.

So, while it's fair to expect some drop-off among African American voters who went to the polls for the unique opportunity of electing the first black president, it's likely that a sizable chunk of those new voters will vote again. And that's good news for the Democratic Party.

The even better news comes from the Hispanic vote. Hispanics are the fastest-growing population in the country. By 2042, a majority of the country will be made up of minorities thanks to that growth. Prior to 2008, the Hispanic vote was generally seen as up for grabs. In broad terms, Hispanic voters are more socially conservative than other Democrats. Those areas of common ground with the Republican Party gave Karl Rove and a handful of other Republican strategists the hope that they might be able to align the Hispanic vote with the Republican Party. It was how Rove largely envisioned the creation of a permanent Republican majority.

In 2004, based in part on the campaign Rove built, 44 percent of Hispanics voted with the Republican Party. That was a nine-point increase over four years, without which Kerry would have surely been elected. Bush won the Southwest and Florida because of that vote margin. While Rove hadn't succeeded in totally realigning Hispanic voters, he'd accomplished enough to assure his boss's reelection. Where he had made inroads, Rove hoped that the next set of Republican leaders would capitalize.

Enter the cast of Republican presidential candidates in 2008. Instead of courting the Hispanic vote, every major Republican candidate actively shunned it. First, there was the immigration reform debate in which Tom Tancredo, a bigoted Colorado congressman and minor presidential candidate, was able to move his whole party wildly to the right. Tancredo ran this ad in Iowa during July 2007:

> Friends, we're losing our country. More than 15 million illegal aliens have invaded our land, placing a massive burden on our schools and hospitals, threatening our security, and turning our country into a bilingual nation. I will build a fence across the entire southern border. I will prosecute employers who hire illegals. I'll make English our official language—and never, ever give amnesty to illegal aliens. I am Tom Tancredo, and I approved this message. Come to the Iowa Straw Poll, and together, let's take our country back.

Yikes.

But while Tancredo's campaign was never taken very seriously, for the summer and fall of 2007 he was able to make immigration a top issue of concern for Republican primary voters. John McCain began to take heat for working on comprehensive immigration reform in the Senate and was slammed over and over by his opponents for sponsoring a bill that allowed the dreaded "amnesty" for undocumented workers. McCain blinked, pulled the legislation, and announced that if he was given a chance to vote on it, he'd vote no, despite having written it in the first place. It was a low, but not the lowest, point of McCain's candidacy.

Conservative radio jumped on the bandwagon. Host Neal Boortz offered this bit of advice in June 2007: "When we yank out the welcome mat, and they all start going back to Mexico, as a going away gift let's all give them a box of nuclear waste. . . . Tell 'em it'll heat tortillas." Rush Limbaugh had joined in a month earlier. He told listeners that when he first met Los Angeles Mayor Antonio Villaraigosa, one of the most prominent Hispanic leaders in the country, he thought he was "either the shoe shine guy or a Secret Service agent."

Soon, other presidential candidates became equally xenophobic, courting their base of conservative voters by lobbing insulting language in the opposite direction. The culmination of their full-on assault on Karl Rove's dream occurred when the top four contenders for the nomination—Mitt Romney, Rudy Giuliani, Fred Thompson, and John McCain—all skipped a debate sponsored by minority groups to discuss minority issues. The minor candidates did attend, flanked on either side by empty podiums with the name plates of those who were missing.

Tavis Smiley, who moderated the debate, was understandably frustrated. "Some of the campaigns who declined our invitations to join us tonight have suggested publicly that this audience would be hostile and unreceptive. Since we are live on PBS right now, I can't tell you what I really think of these kinds of comments." Those candidates who did show up used their opponents' absence as an opportunity to appear more in touch with the minority community.

Mike Huckabee was the most insistent. "I'm embarrassed for our party, and I'm embarrassed for those who did not come," he said, adding that there was a deep division in the country that "doesn't get better when we don't show up." But less than two months later, even Huckabee changed his tune. Afraid he was being outflanked on the anti-immigrant front, Huckabee sought the endorsement of Jim Gilchrist, founder of the Minuteman Project, a group of vigilante border guards. In exchange for the endorsement, Huckabee agreed, among other things, to support one of Gilchrist's pet initiatives, the "anti-anchor baby" amendment. Huckabee promised to support an amendment to the Constitution that would prevent those born in the United States from becoming American citizens automatically, thus depriving the children of undocumented immigrants the chance to be Americans. The pledge was so abhorrent to the Hispanic community, the backlash so loud, that Huckabee had to recant the next day.

As the race marched on, the anti-immigrant language continued, even while immigration dropped off the radar as a top issue of concern for most voters. By the fall of 2008, immigration was no longer a top-five issue, but for Hispanic voters, the debate left a lasting impression.

Mel Martinez, the first Cuban American elected to the Senate and the first Latino to head the Republican National Committee, said on *Meet the Press* in November of 2008, "If Republicans don't figure it out and do the math, we're going to be relegated to minority status. . . . I think that the very divisive rhetoric of the immigration debate set a very bad tone for our brand as Republicans."

By November, Democratic outreach to Hispanic voters, combined with toxic Republican rhetoric, earned Obama a full two-thirds of the Hispanic vote, fourteen points better than John Kerry had received. Karl Rove lamented in a December 2008 *Newsweek* column:

> Hispanics dropped from 44 percent Republican in 2004 to 31 percent in 2008. The GOP won't be a majority party if it cedes the young or Hispanics to Democrats. Republicans must find a way to support secure borders, a guest-worker program and comprehensive immigration reform that strengthens citizenship, grows our economy and keeps America a welcoming nation. An anti-Hispanic attitude is suicidal.

Rove was right. The damage inflicted on Hispanic attitudes toward the Republican Party was severe. In 2004, Bush won New Mexico by two points. In 2008, McCain lost it by fifteen points. In Colorado, there was a thirteen-point swing from Bush's win in 2004 to McCain's loss in 2008, fueled again by a two to one Democratic advantage among Hispanics. And in Nevada, Obama turned the state blue by securing a staggering 76 percent of the Hispanic vote. The combined electoral votes from turning those three states from red to blue was all Obama needed to secure the presidency.

The Hispanic vote is, indeed, a critical key to the Democratic Party maintaining control for a generation. As rightwing conservatives continue to demand nativist language from their politicians and as Republican politicians continue to oblige, the Hispanic vote will continue to solidify as a Democratic stronghold.

The Republicans certainly didn't help themselves during Sonia Sotomayor's confirmation hearings. Over and over again, white Republican men hammered Sotomayor about her infamous "Wise Latina" remark. Earlier in her career, Sotomayor had said that she believed a wise Latina would make a better decision than a white man, based on her set of experiences. How was it possible, they asked, again and again, that she could think a wise Latina would come to a better conclusion than a white man? They grilled her and grilled her, asking questions that had already been answered—only to ask them again. The GOP rejoiced.

But the Hispanic community didn't. Senator Tom Coburn one-upped his pals by reminding Sotomayor, complete with a Ricky Ricardo imitation, that she had "lots of 'splainin' to do." A USA Today poll showed that 42 percent of Hispanics said they would view the Republican Party less favorably if it overwhelmingly opposed the nomination. In the end, that's exactly what happened. Six of the seven Republicans on the Senate Judiciary Committee voted against Sotomayor's confirmation. And on the Senate floor, only nine Republicans voted yes.

Republicans just don't seem to get it. With every year that passes, Hispanic population numbers increase. Those who are already here, but not yet eligible to vote, are becoming citizens at unprecedented levels. In 2008, more than 1 million immigrants were naturalized as U.S. citizens, the most in history. Because of Republican-driven anti-Hispanic rhetoric, these demographic changes will create millions of new Democratic voters over time.

Having Democrats in office over the long haul has the potential to increase Hispanic turnout, as well. Traditionally, Hispanic turnout has been quite low, which is at least partly the product of Republican voter suppression tactics. In October 2006, for example, according to the *Los Angeles Times*, Republican congressional candidate Tan Nguyen sent a Spanish-language letter to around 14,000 Hispanic Democratic voters, warning them not to vote. "Be advised," the letter read, "that if your residence in the United States is illegal or if you are an immigrant, voting in a federal election is a crime that can result in incarceration, and possible deportation for voting without the right to do so." Such efforts spark fears and rumors within Hispanic communities and have in the past contributed to a lackluster turnout.

In 2008, the Mexican American Legal Defense Fund

(MALDEF) filed a federal lawsuit in New Mexico to prevent further voter intimidation. The lead plaintiff was Dora Escobedo, a naturalized citizen who was registered to vote. In the run-up to the 2008 election, Escobedo was harassed at her home by a private investigator. According to MALDEF, the man accused Escobedo of fraudulently registering to vote, claimed she wasn't really a citizen, threatened to call "Immigration," and released her personal information to the public. Escobedo's case isn't unusual. In heavily concentrated Hispanic areas, voter intimidation has become the norm. With it, rumors and misinformation disseminate through the community, convincing many that staying home is simply a safer option than turning out to vote and risking deportation. But that can change over time.

With Democrats gaining steam at the local, state, and federal levels, those who hold office (those in a position to prevent voter intimidation) will be significantly less adversarial to the Hispanic community. If Democratic politicians can convince the community that they need not fear their government, then Democrats can expect to boost Hispanic turnout over time. That must also be coupled with a continuation of policies that support the Hispanic community.

And if the debate over comprehensive immigration reform ever actually results in new, sensible immigration laws, Democrats will surely benefit, both from the resulting new policy and from the inevitable anti-immigrant views Republicans are bound to express during the debate that precedes its passage. Angry town hall protesters of the health care brand showing up to the immigration fight alone could set the party back for an entire generation.

The future success of the Democratic Party is largely driven by the minority vote. If Democratic presidential candidates continue to secure it in such impressive numbers, the party will hold the White House for decades.

Martin Luther King Jr. famously said, "The arc of the universe is long, but it bends toward justice." That has been true throughout history, and it's been progressives who have been doing all the bending. From voting rights to civil rights, from racial integration to women's liberation, the country has always marched forward, however slowly, in the progressive direction. The country is always liberalizing. In 1958, only 4 percent of the country approved of marriage between blacks and whites. Reverend King wouldn't even publicly support it: "I want the white man to be my brother," he offered, "not my brother-in-law." Four years later, the Supreme Court held that laws prohibiting interracial marriage were unconstitutional. Forty-five years later, nearly four out of five Americans think marriage between blacks and whites is perfectly acceptable.

The country changes as it liberalizes. And the political landscape evolves.

Take gay rights, for instance. When Bill Clinton announced his "Don't Ask, Don't Tell" policy, a little more than 50 percent of the country was comfortable with gays serving openly in the military. That number has now climbed to 69 percent. But even more significant, 58 percent of self-described conservatives now favor gays being allowed to openly serve.

In early 2009, as states like Iowa and Vermont were legalizing gay marriage, polls from ABC and CBS showed a dramatic shift in public opinion. For the first time, more Americans were in favor of gay marriage than were opposed, at a margin of 49–46. What was most remarkable was that the shift occurred on both the left and the right. In 2009, three times as many conservatives supported gay marriage as they did in 2004, an unbelievable change in perspective. In only five years, conservatives went from nine in ten opposing gay marriage to nearly one in three supporting it.

Of course, as the GOP continues to falter, a number of those self-described conservatives are no longer self-described Republicans. Among evangelicals, the hardcore base of the party, 75 percent still oppose gay marriage and more than two-thirds say they feel strongly about it. That's what's driving Republican presidential contenders to keep hard-line stances on the issue. And it's another sign of the inevitable undoing of their party. As recently as 2004, gay marriage was a dream political wedge for the Republican Party to use. But as voters continue to become increasingly progressive on the issue, it's a wedge that will only serve to separate the GOP from the rest of the country.

Steve Schmidt, McCain's former campaign manager,

sees the danger. In March 2009, he called on his party to support gay marriage. In an interview with the *Washington Blade,* Schmidt argued that the Republican Party is in danger of permanent damage if it doesn't change its tune. "The attitudes of voters about gay marriage and about domestic partnership benefits for gay couples are changing very rapidly," he noted, "and for voters under the age of 30, they are completely disconnected from what has been Republican orthodoxy on these issues." Schmidt went on to argue that the GOP would lose its moral force if its candidates "go out and try to demonize people on the basis of their sexual orientation." It was wise advice, but as such, it was largely ignored by Republican leaders.

Public perception is changing at an increasingly swift pace, and it's leaving the Republican Party behind. And gay marriage isn't the only issue being swept up in the sea change.

On issues from abortion to marijuana legalization (and even taxes), changing viewpoints are also remaking the political calculus.

While marijuana legalization is still a minority position in the United States, a 2009 ABC poll found that 46 percent now favor its legalization. According to ABC, that was the highest level of support ever recorded, at levels more than twice what they were only twelve years before. And while opposition is still slightly above 50 percent, less than ten years ago, that number was in the midseventies.

On some issues, viewpoints haven't changed particularly dramatically, but the issues themselves have dropped off the radar. Take abortion, for example. While the divide between pro- and anti-choice voters has remained relatively static over the last twenty-five years, the number of voters who cite abortion as an important issue when voting has steadily declined. In 1984, 14 percent of Americans listed abortion as their top issue of concern when choosing their president. By 2006, only 4 percent said it was their top issue. By 2008, only 2 percent said the same, an 85 percent drop over twenty-five years. Even among Republicans, abortion has dropped off the map. In a Fox News poll taken the weekend before the 2008 election, only 11 percent of Republicans said abortion was their top concern. Just 20 percent of Republican women said they would vote only for candidates who shared their view on the issue.

With abortion off the table, the Republicans lose yet another wedge issue. Where ending abortion used to be a rallying cry that could mobilize their base, it's now becoming one that won't effectively mobilize very many at all.

Even the GOP's favorite mantra—"Our taxes are too high!"—is losing ground. Shortly after Obama's middle-class tax cut began showing up in Americans' paychecks, Gallup found that 48 percent of Americans said their tax rates were "about right." That's the second-highest recording of that number since 1956, when Gallup first started collecting the data. These changes in attitudes will continue to have real policy consequences.

Republicans are quickly running out of wedge issues

and will soon find that as time marches on, it will become significantly easier to be a national Democrat and almost impossible to be a nationally viable Republican.

The culture wars have ended. Even the culture warriors know it. James Dobson, founder of Focus on the Family, one of the most powerful institutions on the religious right, resigned as its chairman shortly after Obama's victory. "[W]e made a lot of progress through the eighties," Dobson said in his farewell address, "but then we turned into the nineties and the internet came along and a new president came along and all of that went away and now we are absolutely awash in evil. And we are right now in the most discouraging period of that long conflict. Humanly speaking, we can say that we have lost all those battles."

The influence of the religious right will only diminish further over the years. Millennials hold very progressive views on a host of issues. As they continue to enter the voting population, as their sheer numbers dominate the political process, the nature of political discourse in this country may permanently change. Teixeira notes in his analysis that a full 75 percent of millennials believe there is more that government should be doing. Fifty-eight percent favor gay marriage. Millennials are more progressive on the environment than other generations as well. Only 31 percent think that global warming concerns are exaggerated, while 43 percent of Generation Xers and 47 percent of baby boomers feel the same.

Even young evangelicals are breaking with their

parents. Obama did eight points better among evangelicals under thirty than he did among those over thirty. Though they are still clearly a Republican stronghold, that eight-point gap can have a significant impact on electoral outcomes. Even in its most conservative regions, the country is liberalizing. As time marches on, it can't help but continue to do so.

The consequences of an increasingly progressive America will be sweeping down the line. At the congressional level, more Republican seats will be vulnerable as Democratic voter registration surges in districts in the South, Southwest, and Midwest. Democratic senators and congressmen will see their constituencies shifting leftward. Constituents in districts currently held by Blue Dogs will no longer want such conservative representatives. Senators from once-conservative states will eventually either liberalize or face viable primary challenges from their left. Over time, a wave of progressives will fill the Congress, a reflection of the changing makeup of the American voting population.

As the Democratic caucus in the House and the Senate becomes more progressive, it will also become more unified. In 2009, having sixty Democratic senators didn't guarantee a filibuster-proof majority because a substantial number of Senate Democrats hold viewpoints at odds with the rest of the party. But, in 2020, and in the decades that follow, progressives will be widely represented on Capitol Hill, helping the Democrats to finally begin regularly voting like Republicans—as a unified party. Sixty votes will be easier to get when there are usually sixty senators who agree.

That, in turn, will lead to better policies. Without the need to water down legislation to appease Blue Dogs or moderate Republicans, Democratic proposals will make it through the legislative process more cleanly, with stronger, more comprehensive policies arriving at the president's desk. Better policies will mean better results, and better results will mean happier voters. Progressives will rule the voting booths and will get, in return, a progressive Congress that will produce progressive policies to be signed by a progressive president.

In contrast, the GOP will be completely out of options. Its base will continue to demand that it take far-right stances on all issues. Those who moderate will be punished in primaries. Those who oblige will be unelectable in generals. Either way, Republicans lose. The GOP will still be a major political party. But it will only be successful in sparsely populated rural areas, primarily in the South. Republican candidates will run and lose. And run and lose. And run and lose.

This is what permanent minority status feels like.

And for those in the Republican Party still holding out hope, the only road back to the majority will be to completely transform. Indeed, if the Republicans do make it back to power years from now, their party will be unrecognizable. A progressive country will require a much more progressive party. The GOP will drown if it doesn't embrace that fact. But as long as the Republican Party continues to make campaigns about issues like abortion, gay marriage, traditional family values, religion, and patriotism instead of things like the economy, education, energy, and America's role in the world, it will cease to have influence on the direction of the country.

These population changes will solidify the Democratic permanent majority. In 2016, Obama's successor will run in far more favorable territory than Obama could ever have hoped for. Thirty-two million more millennials will have become eligible voters in those eight years.

During the 2018 midterms, for the first time, the entire millennial generation will be of voting age—an eligible voting population 90 million strong.

According to the U.S. Census Bureau, by 2020, when Obama's successor readies for reelection, the Hispanic community will have grown 40 percent, adding another 25 million to the population. In contrast, the white population will have increased by only 5 percent.

In a country where a full quarter of the population is Hispanic and where 40 percent of voters belong to the millennial generation, it will be difficult for Democrats to lose. And things will only get brighter.

In April of 2020, a new census will be taken, and if the Obama administration and his successor fight for it, that census data will include sampling. When that happens, the redistricting that will follow will include a huge surge in Hispanics—not just because of their population growth, but because sampling will be able to identify those who would otherwise be undercounted.

In 2022, that newly redistricted congressional map will be in use for the first time. The results are sure to tilt the Congress even further to the left.

As the country heads into the 2024 presidential campaign, the Republican Party, under impossibly hostile conditions, will have come to a halt. It will be a small, tired, regional party with little influence on the national stage.

EIGHT

☆ ☆ ☆

Beyond 2020

We did not come here to fear the future. We came here to shape it.

—*Barack Obama*

In 1959, ninety miles south of Miami, Fidel Castro overthrew the U.S.-backed Cuban government. In the aftermath of his rise to power, hundreds of thousands of middle- and upper-class Cubans fled the island, headed for Florida. They arrived on American shores not as immigrants, but as exiles, fully expecting to return to their homeland the moment Castro's regime fell. Between 1959 and 1965, 400,000 Cubans came to Miami. The community there became well established, single-mindedly focused on Cuban issues—so single-minded, in fact, that two decisions made by a Democratic president in the sixties were enough to turn the entire community into a generation of Republicans.

In 1961, the Kennedy administration trained Cuban refugees for a mission to overthrow Castro. When they arrived at the Bay of Pigs, Castro and his army, who had been tipped off, were ready for them. The attack failed; hundreds of Cuban refugees were slaughtered. It was a foreign policy blunder on a number of fronts; for the Cuban population, it was seen as a serious betrayal.

Then came the Cuban missile crisis. For nearly two weeks in October, President Kennedy faced off with the Soviet Union in a nuclear test that brought the two nations closer to total destruction than at any other time in history. Nikita Khrushchev had placed Soviet missiles in Cuba that were close enough to the United States to give the Soviet Union first-strike capability. It was an incredibly destabilizing move. A chess game unfolded between the United States and the Soviets, complete with a U.S. naval blockade of Cuba and a number of threatening communications between the countries.

In the end, Kennedy and Khrushchev made a pact. Khrushchev would dismantle the weapons in Cuba and then, a number of months down the line, Kennedy would take down similar U.S. missiles in Turkey (the United States had planned to remove them anyway). But that wasn't the part of the negotiation that infuriated Cubans living in America. Khrushchev sent Kennedy a letter demanding that the United States "respect the inviolability of Cuban borders and its sovereignty, pledge not to interfere in internal affairs, not to invade Cuba itself or make its territory available as a bridgehead for such an invasion, and . . . restrain those who might contemplate committing aggression against Cuba, either from U.S. territory or from the territory of Cuba's neighboring states." In other words, the United States would have to promise not to invade Cuba, thus solidifying Castro's position as immovable dictator of the country. Kennedy agreed.

The Cuban community was irreconcilably furious. Still today, while John Kennedy's name garners universal respect and admiration in most parts of the country, it continues to be a dirty word in Miami. Cuban exiles began to cope with their new reality: Castro's regime would not be ending anytime soon. They held out hope for another decade or so, with most still considering themselves exiles in America. But as the sixties turned into the seventies, many Cubans began thinking of themselves as Cuban Americans. In 1973, 60 percent of Cuban exiles expressed an intention of returning to Cuba after the fall of Castro. By 1979, only 25 percent felt the same. Between 1970 and 1980, more than half of all Cuban exiles had applied for citizenship.

By the time Carter was seeking reelection, that made the newly naturalized Cuban community in Miami a serious political force. They were heavily courted by Ronald Reagan, who won more than 70 percent of their support. Four years later, they delivered him similar margins. But it wasn't until the 2000 election that the public at large began to understand the weight and influence the Cuban vote carried. Reagan had won their votes, but he also won forty states in 1980 and forty-nine in 1984. Cuban Americans had nothing to do with the outcome of those elections. But in 2000, the Cuban population almost single-handedly gave the White House to George W. Bush.

In response to the Elián González controversy, in which President Clinton ordered the young refugee returned to his father in Cuba, Cuban Americans voted overwhelmingly against the Democratic Party. George W. Bush won 82 percent of the Cuban vote (out of about 450,000 that were cast). That was a net gain of around 288,000 votes for Bush in a state he ended up winning after an infamous recount by only 537 votes. Had Bush won only 81 percent of the Cuban vote instead of 82, Al Gore would have taken Florida and, with it, the White House.

But as the country transforms itself, the Cuban community is not immune. The liberalization of the country is happening in Miami just as it is everywhere else. Younger Cuban Americans—those who were born in the United States or who arrived here as children—tend to have a different outlook on American politics than their parents and grandparents. They are less Cuba-centric in their ideology, and while they are less progressive than their political generational counterparts, they are significantly more progressive than the Cuban community has been in the past.

Obama received only 35 percent of the Cuban vote, but that was still the highest percentage ever recorded by a Democrat. And the breakdown by generation was telling. Among Cuban voters under forty-five years old, a majority, 51 percent, voted for Obama. Among voters over sixty-five, 80 percent voted for John McCain.

Even among those who still consider themselves staunch Republicans, an evolution of ideology is well under way. In 2006, only half of Cuban Americans supported changing the law to permit all American citizens unrestricted travel to Cuba. Just three years later, 67 percent felt the same way. Sixty-four percent of Cubans approved of Obama's Cuba policy, which allows Cuban Americans a broader ability to travel to Cuba and transfer money to immediate family members. In fact, at the time that Obama announced his policy, about two-thirds of Cubans said they approved of his job performance, an unprecedented show of support for a Democratic president and a traditionally Democratic policy.

The Cuban vote is changing. Over time, younger, American-born Cubans are replacing their exiled grandparents in the voting pool. They are more likely to be driven by economic and social concerns than by an exclusively anti-Castro outlook. By 2024, the youngest of those senior citizens who voted overwhelmingly for John McCain will be in their eighties. In not much time, the Cuban vote will cease to be the Republican king-making force of statewide politics in Florida.

In an ever-growing, ever-liberalizing population, the Cuban community will become Democratic. And in the meantime, it will be dwarfed by an influx of non-Cuban Hispanic voters. In 1990, Cuban Americans made up almost half of the Hispanic vote in Florida. By 2008, they composed only a third. The influx of non-Cuban Hispanics in Florida is part of what's turning the state blue. Obama won 70 percent of the non-Cuban Hispanic vote in Florida during the 2008 election. That was on the heels of a massive voter registration drive in which Democratic registration went up by 38 percent (compared to only 7 percent for Republicans). The result: For the first time since the data was recorded, Democratic Hispanics outnumbered Republican Hispanics in Florida.

All of these trends are expected to continue. And the combination of these trends means that Florida will be among a number of critical states that are fading from the battleground.

As the Cuban American vote liberalizes over time and as the non-Cuban Hispanic population swells, Florida will slowly become a Democratic stronghold. Like Pennsylvania and Michigan, it will probably still be heavily contested by the Republican Party; but over the long term, it's unlikely that the GOP will retake it.

By 2016, Florida will seem out of reach for Republicans. By 2024, it will be solidly Democratic. Consider the implications: Had Florida always been a Democratic stronghold, the Democrats would have held the White House continuously for the last eighteen years. Florida is the fourth most populous state; its twenty-seven electoral votes are so critical to a Republican majority that without them, there is essentially no path back to the White House.

In 2008, we already saw what this kind of shift could

mean. Obama did twenty-seven points better among Hispanics than John Kerry. In 2004, Kerry lost by more than
400,000 votes in Florida. Obama won by 240,000. Each
year, each time a Democratic candidate runs for president,
that Florida margin will be easier and easier to achieve.
Over time, it could very well spell the end of Republican
presidential politics.

And the hemorrhaging doesn't stop there.

Don't look now, but Texas, home to George W. Bush
and big oil, home to a school system that banned Thomas
Jefferson, a state that kills more inmates than any other,
a state that sports a secessionist governor, is rapidly turning blue.

It's happening—and fast—though for some on the
ground, it's really not all that surprising. After all, Texas
wasn't always a red state.

Lyndon Johnson helped carry Texas for John Kennedy
and won it himself when he ran for president in 1964. In
1968, Texas voted for Hubert Humphrey and in 1976, for
Jimmy Carter. Even when George H. W. Bush was at his
most popular as president, Democrat Ann Richards was
elected governor of Texas. But by the time George W. Bush
defeated Richards, the pendulum of Texas politics had
swung firmly back in the Republican direction.

In 1980, Reagan won 55 percent of the vote in Texas.
In 1984, he won 63 percent. By the time George W. Bush
was running for president as Texas's favorite son (despite,
of course, having grown up, not in Texas, but among the
whitest crust of the Connecticut elite), Texas was voting

Republican at incredibly consistent rates. Bush took 60 percent of the vote in the 2000 presidential election and 61 percent in 2004.

At the state level, the political scene looks just as hopeless for the Democratic Party. Republicans now control both chambers of the state legislature and all statewide elected positions. In the upcoming 2010 gubernatorial race, Rick Perry is heavily favored.

But while things may look and seem the same, the political landscape is shifting dramatically. While the battle for the governor's mansion soaks up the focus of the media, a quieter but equally relevant battle will be brewing. Democrats will be trying to retake the state house for the first time since 2002. After the 2008 election, they are only two seats away from that goal.

But what's happening in the short term is nothing compared to the transformation that is occurring within the Texas electorate over time.

Texas is the fastest-growing state in the country. Every year, hundreds of thousands of people move into the state, mostly into urban centers like Houston, Austin, San Antonio, and Dallas. Houston is growing at such a high rate that, according to the *Economist,* it is projected to move up a slot from fourth-largest city in the country to third.

As of 2009, only four states in the country are majority-minority states (meaning a majority of the population is made up of minorities). Texas has been one since 2004.

The Census Bureau projects that by 2015, Hispanics will be the largest ethnic group in the state, outpacing its substantial growth in other parts of the country. What is happening around the country is happening more quickly in Texas, and the results are bound to cause problems for the Republican Party.

Like elsewhere in the country, the Texas Hispanic vote went largely to Barack Obama, who garnered 63 percent of their support. Hispanics also increased their turnout rate by a considerable 3 percent between 2004 and 2008 (though it still lagged significantly behind white voters in Texas). As their numbers continue to grow, the political calculus of Texas will shift.

When Obama's successor runs for president in 2016, Hispanics will be more dominant than any other ethnic group in the state, including whites. As those changes progress, the Democratic Party in Texas will further evolve into a Hispanic-centric operation. Already, the Mexican American Legislative Caucus is the dominant core of the legislature's Democratic caucus. Increases in population will only lead to increases in Hispanic Democrats serving in public office. Over time, that dominance will translate into a significant tightening of the partisan gap. No longer will Texas be left uncontested by the Democrats at the presidential level; no longer will it be a shoe-in victory for any statewide politician with an "R" in front of his or her name.

But it's not just Hispanic population growth that is

fueling the turning tide in Texas. It's also urban growth. Most of the population surge occurring in Texas is happening in the heart of its urban centers, where Democrats have traditionally outperformed Republicans.

Houston, for example, is experiencing incredible growth—between 2007 and 2008, the Houston metropolitan area added about 130,000 new residents. It has seen its population grow more than 38 percent since 1990. That growth is attributable to a number of factors: The Houston economy withstood the recession better than most other places in the country. It continues to be the self-proclaimed energy capital of the world and offers thousands of jobs for skilled laborers and highly educated professionals. Next to energy, NASA also provides a huge job market in the area, covering over 20,000 Houston-area jobs. And, while it has as much to offer as the country's other big cities, it is uncommonly cheap to live there.

That kind of growth changes a political landscape. The city just elected an openly gay mayor, the first of any major city in the country. And what's more is that, of the major competitors in the race, the only serious contenders were Democrats. For the first time since Jimmy Carter's 1976 campaign, Harris County, which includes Houston, voted for the Democratic candidate for president in 2008. In fact, similar growth in other urban centers helped Obama win all the big cities in Texas except for Fort Worth.

He won in Austin, which had the highest rate of growth of any metro area in 2008, and which is about as distinct from George W. Bush's Texas as is possible to contemplate. Austin is the East Village of the South, as if New York and Los Angeles had a raunchy one-night stand and produced a strangely perfect love child—only to let it be raised by a foster parent with a drinking problem.

But Obama won outside of Austin, too. He won in Dallas, which isn't at all like Austin—more like Houston's classier older sister. He won El Paso and San Antonio, too, all without ever bothering to compete in Texas during the general election. Obama did spend time in Texas during the primary while he was still fighting Hillary Clinton for the nomination, but as soon as he turned to general election mode, Texas was entirely off his radar. Well, not entirely. He did show up once to a fundraiser in the ritzy River Oaks community of Houston. But, beyond that, he never campaigned in Texas. He put a token number of staff on the ground, recruiting volunteers in Texas only to drive them to the competitive race in New Mexico. The campaign quickly wrote off his chances. Still, even with that posture, Obama only lost Texas by eleven points. Four years earlier, John Kerry lost by twenty-three.

Where Texas is growing, Democrats are winning. And where Republicans are winning, the state is in decline. Republicans can count on rural voters to support them, but each year, the rural population is decreasing. Even in a state like Texas, Republican strongholds are diminishing rapidly.

The electoral consequences going forward are substantial. Over the next few election cycles, Texas will inevitably become more competitive. Growth in the four years of

Obama's presidency might even convince his reelection campaign operatives to make serious investments there. As Texas transforms into a battleground state, the Republican Party will find itself playing defense in one of the most expensive states in the country. Saturating the airwaves of Texas's twenty-two media markets with political ads can cost as much as $2 million each week. That's money that Republicans would much prefer to spend elsewhere. Instead, they'll have to funnel it into Texas, no longer the lock it once was.

Over time, there is a Democratic inevitability brewing in Texas. As the Hispanic population continues to grow at dramatic rates and as the populations of the state continue to move into urban areas, Texas will suddenly, but not surprisingly, turn blue at the presidential level and below.

When that happens, when Democrats start winning Texas again, the Republican Party will be lost. Texas is second only to California in its number of electoral votes. Making up for losing Texas would require a big Republican win in the golden state; but by then, California, like Texas, will have become majority-minority. Over time, it will become more progressive, not less.

The loss of Texas from the Republican map, like the loss of Florida, can stand on its own in terms of detriment to the party. The loss of either state means the Republican Party will lack any path to a majority of electoral votes. The loss of both will only underscore that blistering reality.

A similar story will echo in other states, as well. In the

Southwest, Colorado, New Mexico, and Nevada will continue to trend Democratic, while Arizona moves closer, on a wave of Hispanic growth, to joining them. In Virginia and North Carolina, much like in Texas, large population increases in key metropolitan areas will fuel an increased progressivism and solidify those states as permanent battlegrounds.

Beyond 2020, the impact of these changes will be irrefutable. In 2008, part of the Obama campaign's strategy was to expand the map on which they forced John McCain to compete. By spreading out the playing field and forcing McCain to play defense in unexpected places, Obama managed to weaken him everywhere. That same dynamic will play out in 2020, though the map will already be safely in Democratic hands. It will be spread so wide, with comfortable Democratic margins in so many places, that the GOP will have few places where they can compete.

Like McCain, Republicans will try to play offense in Democratic areas. They'll show up in Pennsylvania and Michigan and in parts of the Midwest, but the poll numbers will never show up with them. Unless the party entirely reinvents itself, it will run aground in countless elections at all levels of government. If it doesn't transform completely, it will continue to devolve into nothing more than a southern, rural faction.

That's why the next ten years are so critical. Beyond 2020, everything falls into place especially well for the Democratic Party. The progressive millennials, the growing

Hispanic vote, and the liberalization of the voting public illuminate a promising liberal future. With the Republican Party unable to compete at a national level, with the White House locked up and the Congress shifting leftward, it suddenly becomes much easier to argue that the Democrats could be in power for the full twenty-four-year generation.

Beyond 2020, everything changes.

If the Republican Party is unable to get up off the mat, it makes sense to wonder whether a third party will emerge in its place. After all, the Republican Party itself supplanted the Whig Party, which collapsed under irreconcilable differences among interparty factions. There are precedents for new parties emerging out of nowhere.

While Teddy Roosevelt was president, he loved William Howard Taft, thought he'd make a perfect successor. They saw eye to eye on policy, Roosevelt thought, and Taft had performed impressively as secretary of war. As a result, he hand-picked Taft to succeed him.

But while president, Taft had a way of infuriating allies and enemies alike. By the end of his term, he'd alienated the entire party establishment, including Roosevelt himself. In fact, Roosevelt was so furious with his former protégé that he created a third party, the Bull Moose Party, and declared his intention to challenge Taft for the presidency.

In the history of third parties, this was a pretty big

deal. A well-loved, well-respected former president created his own party to take back the White House from his unpopular replacement. It was, from the perspective of observers of the time, a very serious contest.

Roosevelt campaigned feverishly, traveling all around the country. One October night in 1912, as he was preparing to give a speech, a would-be assassin lunged toward the former president and fired at his chest from close range. Roosevelt fell back as he felt the bullet penetrate. Dazed, he reached into his pocket to find that the bullet had been slowed when it first hit the notes for the speech he had intended to give. The bullet still pierced the president, but not fatally. Though he was losing blood, he got up and began to deliver the speech.

"Friends," Roosevelt announced to his cheering audience as he held up the tattered speech, "it takes more than that to kill a Bull Moose!"

It was a pretty macho moment—really the best kind of American political theater. Teddy Roosevelt—the guy they named the teddy bear after, the guy you know from popular American treasures like Mount Rushmore and Yosemite, that Teddy Roosevelt, that guy actually got up and delivered his speech with a bullet still in his chest. It really happened—just like that.

In the end, Roosevelt was right—a bullet wouldn't take down the Bull Moose Party. But an American election would.

Roosevelt, it turned out, hadn't created a new constituency with his third party. He just split the Republicans in half. In November 1912, he walked away with 27 percent of the vote to Taft's 23. Together, they would have had a majority of the country. But divided, they allowed Woodrow Wilson to win the presidency with only 41 percent of the vote.

It's been the same basic story since.

In 1948, a group of southern Democrats, furious that President Truman supported anti-segregationist policies, walked out of the Democratic Convention to form a third party, the Dixiecrats. Their platform called for a continued segregation of American society:

> We stand for the segregation of the races and the racial integrity of each race; the constitutional right to choose one's associates . . . We oppose the elimination of segregation, the repeal of miscegenation statutes, the control of private employment by Federal bureaucrats called for by the misnamed civil rights program. We favor home-rule, local self government, and a minimum interference with individual rights.

At the same convention where they adopted those words, they selected South Carolina Governor Strom Thurmond as their presidential nominee. Thurmond and the Dixiecrats had hoped to siphon enough votes from the South to prevent either Harry Truman or Thomas Dewey from getting a majority of electoral votes. (If a president doesn't get an electoral vote majority, the House of Representatives gets to pick the president.) Their expectation was that if the Dixiecrats could win all 127 southern state electoral votes, they'd have enough leverage in the House to prevent civil rights policies from being enacted.

From the beginning, the Dixiecrats knew that a third party had no chance of actually winning the White House. The political mechanics were impossible. But even accepting their role as spoiler, as a strictly regional party, the Dixiecrats failed to reach their goal. Thurmond carried only four states and 39 electoral votes, not the 127 he had hoped for. The rest of the South voted for Truman.

Twenty years later, Alabama Governor George Wallace tried the same thing, this time as the leader of the American Independent Party. He did slightly better than Thurmond, winning five states and forty-six electoral votes. But like Thurmond, his presence on the ballot had little impact on the ultimate outcome of the race.

Third parties face huge mechanical problems. When Ross Perot ran in 1992, he received more popular votes than any third-party candidate in history. But with it came zero electoral college votes. Unlike Wallace and Thurmond, Perot was not a regionally specific candidate. He was able to receive popular support in every state in the union. But in a winner-take-all electoral college system, placing third is worth nothing. So while his support may have been broad, it was simply too shallow to ever show up on the scoreboard.

Even when the Republican Party is at its weakest, the idea that a third party could emerge to supplant it is unrealistic. Historically, it's true, parties have come and gone out of existence. But the difference in operation and infrastructure, in what it means to be a major national party, is so dramatic now that present and past are really not analogous.

The Republican Party is a massive operation, the equivalent of a multibillion-dollar national corporate conglomerate. Any emerging third party is, comparably, like a small chain of mediocre tapas restaurants. There is simply no way to compete.

Even as the Tea Party emerges as a credible force on the right, there is no realistic chance of a Tea Party candidate winning the presidency or of a Tea Party caucus taking control of the House or Senate. The coalition challenges are insurmountable. No third-party challenge from the far right (or the far left) could garner enough support among mainstream voters to become truly competitive on the national stage.

In the meantime, the Republicans will be facing some impossible choices.

They can try to moderate, become a more classically Libertarian-style party, and adopt a hands-off policy on both economic and social issues. Doing that might attract Independent voters—even some Democrats who only vote with their party because they are socially liberal. But doing so will mean abandoning the far-right base, which, in turn, will mean a huge loss in organizational capacity—and votes. It's the base that volunteers, that gives small donations, and shows up to vote. Without them, the party will have formed a new, weaker coalition, still too small to win a national election.

It really doesn't matter how divorced members of the far right become from the rest of the country. There are still far too many for the Republican Party to write them off.

Of course, when they don't ignore the right, they end up ignoring just about everyone else. It's an enormous challenge, perhaps an insurmountable one, and it will be faced by a party that rarely exhibits the ability to make hard choices.

It may well be that the best hope for the Republican Party lies in the next ten years. Look behind you at the journey we've taken so far. In the next ten years, much of what propels the Democratic Party is tactical. It's a function of persevering through midterm elections, capitalizing on the redistricting process, and getting a once-in-a-generation president reelected. It's about finding his successor and keeping the country focused on the success of a progressive agenda.

After that, Democratic success is a function of something different entirely—seismic demographic shifts, a new outlook of a new generation, and a realignment of the Hispanic community. If Republicans haven't derailed the Democratic Party by then, they'll be out of reasonable options.

Which isn't to say that taking down the Democratic Party in the next ten years will be easy. We've already seen the enormous advantages the Democrats hold and the political realities that will continue to fuel their success. While the party looks especially strong, comparatively, the next ten years will be its most vulnerable. And that's why it's critical that the party, from the average voter to the active volunteer to the Congress and White House, capitalize on all the coming advantages throughout the next decade. We have to survive the upcoming midterms, battle aggressively during the redistricting process, continue to build on infrastructure investments, and work as tirelessly as we did in 2008 to ensure the president's reelection. Then, we have to mobilize behind the right successor.

The bottom line is that the Republicans' best hope for stopping the Democratic Party lies just ahead. If today's Democrats can get the job done, tomorrow's will enjoy a permanent majority. Because beyond 2020, we're home free.

NINE

☆ ☆ ☆

The Hard Part

When you get too big a majority, you're immediately in trouble.

—*Sam Rayburn*

Early January 2005 was a pretty rough time to be a Democrat. President George W. Bush was going to continue to be President George W. Bush for another four years. The right wing was more excited than it had been since the Ronald Reagan bobble-head doll had gone on sale. Karl Rove's enthusiasm for a possible permanent majority was boiling over, just as the president readied himself for his second inaugural. Democrats felt defeated, were defeated, and for most, a path out of the darkness seemed impossibly blocked.

It was under those conditions that Nancy Pelosi called Rahm Emanuel and asked him to chair the Democratic effort to take back the House of Representatives. The job seemed like quite the uphill battle: They'd need to knock off a number of Republican incumbents to pick up the fifteen seats needed, and they would have to do so at a time when incumbents appeared particularly secure in their positions. But Emanuel seemed the perfect person for the job. He'd been a top political lieutenant in the Clinton White House and an executive director of the Democratic Congressional Campaign Committee (DCCC), the same operation he was now being asked to chair. He was a national fundraiser for Clinton's campaign and had a strong set of national contacts. He also had a keen sense of smart, and sometimes ruthless, campaign strategy.

Emanuel approached the national campaign differently from those who'd preceded him. First, he recruited a number of very conservative Democrats—people who were perfectly suited for the districts they were competing in but who objected to significant portions of the Democratic platform. "Some people argue about old Democrats and new Democrats," Emanuel said at a January 2005 news conference after being named to his new post. "I'm a Vince Lombardi Democrat. Winning is everything."

Winning was, indeed, everything to Emanuel. In places where Democrats had never been able to compete, winning meant recruiting candidates who were pro-life and pro-gun, who defined themselves as fiscal conservatives. Recruits included businessmen, farmers, former military, and former Republicans. In *The Thumpin'*, author Naftali Bendavid recounts how Chris Van Hollen, Emanuel's number two at the DCCC and the man who would chair the committee's 2008 effort, described their simple recruiting philosophy:

> This is not a theoretical exercise. The goal is to win this thing. In dealing with candidates, we don't have an ideological purity test. If you believe in the basic gut principles of the Democratic party—opportunity, fairness for all—we're not going to hold people to a litmus test on a checklist of issues that certain interest groups may have an interest in.

Given the diversity in ideology among Democrats nationally, Emanuel treated each race individually, learning the intricacies of each neighborhood in each key district, what was working on the ground and what wasn't. According to a November 2006 *Chicago Tribune* article, James Carville and Stan Greenberg, who were instrumental in getting Bill Clinton elected and who were close friends of Emanuel, pushed aggressively for Emanuel to have all Democratic campaigns shift to a strictly positive message in the last weeks of the 2006 race. But Emanuel resisted. "James!" he shouted during one reported phone call. "No, James, you listen! Can you listen for one fucking minute? I'm working these campaigns all the time. The campaigns all have different textures." He had been deeply involved in each race, understood the different dynamics playing out in each district, and refused to paint them with such a broad and superficial brush.

That decision paid off. He lost fourteen pounds in the

process, but in the end, he received the lion's share of credit for the Democrats picking up thirty-one seats in the House and taking back the majority for the first time in twelve years. Two years later, Van Hollen ran a similar operation, and on the coattails of the massive Obama organization, helped elect another twenty-one Democrats.

Winning those seats meant a healthy Democratic majority—a security in numbers. But it wasn't without consequences.

Enter the Blue Dogs.

In 1995, a group of conservative Democrats formed an alliance in the House, a relatively common way to build increased influence on Capitol Hill. In a chamber with 435 members, any single congressperson has relatively little power outside of any chairmanships or leadership positions. But forming a caucus, assembling a group of members who are willing to vote as a bloc, can help increase the ability of an otherwise marginalized group to be heard. In this case, a group of Democrats from right-leaning districts joined together to form the Blue Dogs. There is some dispute over the origin of the name. It's partly an homage to the Yellow Dogs, a group of southern Democrats who opposed their party's view on issues like segregation and civil rights, but who refused to join a political party founded by Lincoln. Some Blue Dogs have described the color choice as a function of being squeezed so hard to toe the party line that they've turned blue.

Whatever the origin, the outcome was the same—a newly formed coalition of conservative Democrats sought to ensure that they weren't railroaded by progressives. Two years later, another group, the New Democrat Coalition, was founded. Like the Blue Dogs, the New Democrats fancied themselves as fiscally conservative on economic issues. But unlike the Blue Dogs, who tended to also hold socially conservative views, the New Democrats are primarily socially liberal.

After Emanuel's impressive 2006 victory, forty-two new Democratic freshmen were elected. More than half joined the Blue Dogs or the New Democrats. Two years later, of the thirty-five freshman Democrats, nearly three in four joined at least one of the two coalitions.

The wins were critical for the party; the Democrats retook control of the House. But while the outcome helped liberalize the Congress as a whole, it was a moderating force on the Democratic caucus itself. The House Democrats now included fifty-two Blue Dogs and New Democrats. Those members also happened to be the most vulnerable to electoral defeat.

The same basic story played out in almost every conservative district in which the Democrats won. For years, a Republican holds the seat. Other Republican politicians in the area, itching to move up the ladder, wait patiently, though with frustration, for that member of Congress to finally retire so they can have a shot at the big show. They wait and wait, continuing to build their network of contacts and base of power, counting down the years before it's finally their turn. Then, seemingly out of the blue, the guy they've been praying would finally retire gets beaten in an upset by one of Rahm Emanuel's conservative Democrat recruits.

For most in the GOP, the news isn't good. But for those who have long held the private ambition of being their district's next congressperson, the opportunity is a golden one. With no Republican incumbent in their way, those who've been in the on-deck circle for years are finally up at bat. This is what makes the life of a Blue Dog Democrat so impossibly driven with electoral paranoia.

From the moment they get elected (often in districts that Democrats have no business winning in), they are under siege. Every day is about fundraising for the next election. Every legislative decision is weighed in terms of how angry constituents might get. It is a constant struggle between toeing the party line and showing enough independence to avoid being branded at home as "just another liberal Democrat."

In order to preserve their majority, Nancy Pelosi and the rest of the Democratic leadership reached out to the conservative freshmen immediately. They were given free rein to vote against the party when necessary to protect their political viability, and they were offered prime seats on highly coveted committees, positions usually reserved for more senior members.

Of course, protecting such a diverse majority is not without consequences. The Energy and Commerce Committee was among those that offered seats to vulnerable members. It was also a key committee in charge of producing health care legislation in 2009. Blue Dogs on the committee opposed aspects of the health care bill, largely over fears that it would be unpopular back home. Given the size of their cohort, Henry Waxman, chairman of the committee, was forced to cut a deal with them. For a while, Waxman and the Blue Dogs were at what seemed like an impossible impasse. Things looked so ugly that Waxman actually floated the idea of bypassing his own committee to avoid having to compromise. Upon hearing that news, the full Blue Dog coalition put out a statement threatening to oppose the legislation from the floor en masse. Their influence simply couldn't be ignored.

Over the long term, this kind of swollen majority will present one of the most significant challenges to Democratic dominance. As much as progressives would like to think otherwise, building a Democratic majority requires electing those who don't subscribe to every prong of the Democratic agenda. The result is a largely factional party that has to be wrangled together to produce enough votes to get anything done. This leaves the party in a rather perilous position at times. Compromise on legislation infuriates the left, but without compromise, substantive legislative accomplishments are usually impossible.

That calculus also corners Blue Dogs and other conservative Democrats into a difficult paradox: If they don't challenge aspects of Obama's agenda, they'll risk being seen as too far to the left of their district. But if they derail major pieces of legislation and, as a result, hurt the Democratic Party's popularity, they will be among the first to lose their seats.

Over the long haul, this careful dance between the factions of the Democratic Party will be a substantial challenge to building a permanent majority. If the intra-party battle results in paralysis, if the Democrats are incapable of producing substantive policy because either Blue Dogs or progressives refuse to compromise, that inaction will give the appearance—the accurate appearance—that the Democratic Party is incapable of governing.

So how do they get this one right? The strategy that evolves has to be one that recognizes that at the end of the day, success in congressional elections requires that the Congress actually produces legislation the president can sign. That means that legislative compromises will almost always be more valuable for the party politically than allowing bills to die on principle. Over time, as the country continues to liberalize, this will get a lot easier. Many conservative districts will shift leftward, allowing Blue Dogs to vote with the party more often and with less fear of political retribution. But, in the meantime, the future of the Democratic Party is dependent, in large part, on the ability of an ideologically diverse Democratic caucus to seek out common ground consistently. That can mean things like adopting an "all-of-the-above" approach to energy policy— one that satisfies the left by curbing global warming emissions, but that also satisfies moderates by increasing domestic production of oil and gas. Or, as we saw momentarily during the health care debate, it can mean providing a progressive policy option, but allowing individual states—and with them, vulnerable legislators—to opt out.

Of course, the Blue Dogs won't be the only challenge the Democratic Party faces. While some will be focused on compromise within the party, others will continue their obsession with building bipartisanship.

The American voting public loves that word. Bipartisanship. It sounds so civil, so reasonable. Obama ran on a platform that urged us to forget about blue states and red states, to see ourselves as one nation and one people.

But the desire for bipartisanship can be awfully dangerous at a time when the Republican Party continues to operate as a dysfunctional fringe group. During the first month of Obama's presidency, his administration put a premium on passing an economic stimulus package in a bipartisan fashion. Talking points coming out of the White House focused on the Obama administration's desire to work with Republicans on the Hill to pass a substantive bill. Negotiations included courting key Republican votes and making a battery of significant compromises to the size and scope of the legislation.

In the end, with the exception of three Republicans in the Senate (one of whom switched parties soon thereafter), the GOP voted in unified opposition to the stimulus package. It had decided on a strategy that meant it would oppose the Obama administration on all issues, at all times—whatever the cost, whatever the outcome. And because it was the administration that had been pushing for a bipartisan solution, the GOP was able to paint the president as the person responsible for failing to bring both parties together.

Of course, at the time, the political hit was relatively minor—Obama's approval numbers stayed in the high sixties for months. And, eventually, as the stimulus begins to show its undeniably positive impact on the economy, the Republicans will find themselves on the wrong side of the issue. But the broader point is a critical one for both the administration and for the Democratic leadership on the Hill to recognize: As the GOP unravels, Democrats must avoid the temptation of bipartisanship.

For one thing, it breathes life into a party that doesn't deserve our help. The Republicans will continue to be seen as an unacceptable alternative as long as they refuse to engage in the process.

And as time goes on, corralling bipartisan support for any initiative of value will become increasingly difficult. While the country liberalizes and as the Republican base becomes further divorced from the ideological outlook of the rest of the nation, Republican elected officials will continue to shift rightward. It took almost no time for Republican congressmen to question the president's citizenship, for example. All they needed were the crazies at home to start it. That isn't going to change, and the result will surely be a Republican Party that is impossible to negotiate with.

If Democrats continue to talk about bipartisanship as a normative value, as something we ought to be aiming for, they will increase in importance the very thing they have the least control over. By definition, bipartisanship requires action on the part of the minority; unless the GOP sees a political advantage to signing onto legislation, it simply will not do it. And the party that promised bipartisanship will be the one to blame. That's just bad politics, and, over the long term, it could inflict lasting damage.

Instead, the Democrats should put their focus, simply enough, on crafting smart policies that align with the views and values of the public at large—without regard for bipartisanship. Over time, that will only underscore the irrelevance of the Republican Party and will produce popular legislation at the same time. It's easier, it's faster, and it's better politics.

During the 2008 campaign, Democrats were buzzing about the far-off possibility that they might just win enough seats in the Senate to earn a filibuster-proof majority. The stars had to align in a pretty extraordinary way: a *Saturday Night Live* comedian would have to get elected in Minnesota. A Democrat would have to beat Ted Stevens in Alaska, who'd held office for forty years. Seven others would also have to turn red seats blue. In the end, they came incredibly close. Al Franken pulled off his win by just over 300 votes (and after six months of court appeals). Ted Stevens was indicted on federal corruption charges. The party ended up just one vote shy of that sixty-vote threshold. That is, until Arlen Specter switched seats.

Facing a primary challenge from the right, Specter switched to the Democratic Party and, in doing so, secured a sixty-seat majority for the party. Most Democrats were thrilled—finally, the Republicans couldn't stand in our way, they cheered. Finally, the Republicans would be unable to filibuster so many critical bills on the floor of the Senate. But there was another, smaller group of Democrats, perhaps more cynical, perhaps more realistic, who collectively gulped upon hearing the news. With a filibuster-proof majority, the Democrats would face an entirely new paradigm:

All the blame. All the credit.

These folks knew all too well that inaction in the Senate wasn't the exclusive result of the Republican filibuster. It was as much a function of conservative Democrats warring within their party. After Democrats retook the Senate in 2006, disagreement among them on how to approach the war in Iraq was evidence of just how badly hamstrung the party could be. Still, when confronted and criticized, Democratic congressional leaders had what felt like a reasonable excuse. They had control of the Senate, yes, but the Republican Party had control over the filibuster. Without sixty votes, there was nothing the Democrats could do, they explained—nothing to prevent Republican obstruction.

With fifty-nine votes in the Senate, even with a large majority in the House and Obama in the White House, the Democrats could still argue, whenever they had to, that any and all failures were the product of the GOP. The reality is, with sixty votes, the calculus in the Senate doesn't actually change all that much—the Democrats are still not unified enough to easily corral all sixty on a controversial piece of legislation. Nonetheless, with that sixtieth seat, the narrative changed.

The Democrats had no one to blame but themselves for inaction. They'd lost a key talking point—a key way of defending their shortcomings. It is true that with their new power came the lion's share of the credit for good policy. Democrats own the economic recovery. But with the credit comes the potential for blame. Where the government fails, only Democrats are accountable.

Democrats lost their sixtieth vote in early 2010. But when they get it back—as they one day will—the challenges that come with it will be the same.

There is no easy answer to this challenge, except to say this: In a democracy, power is earned. The Democratic Party will not build a permanent majority without having deserved to. If the party doesn't govern effectively in Congress, it will eventually lose.

Nevertheless, the circumstances the party finds itself in are the most favorable it could ask for. As the public continues to become more progressive and as Congress begins to reflect that changing viewpoint, governing will get easier. The party will be more unified around policies that the public will increasingly favor. The GOP will continue to obsess over the needs of its base, furthering its own unraveling. But even under those circumstances, the Democrats can lose it all.

American elections offer a binary choice. There are only two viable parties to choose from. Even when one party proves itself to be an unreasonable alternative, it will continue to be the only alternative available. If Democrats lose control of their agenda, if their message isn't backed up with concrete results that average voters can understand and appreciate, the Republican Party will have a chance to reemerge. And though the underlying dynamics of the American political landscape will still dramatically favor the Democrats, the party will not be entirely impervious to the kind of wave election that brought Republicans back to power in 1994. Such a resurgence would likely be short-lived, but as the Democrats learned during the last decade, a lot of damage can be done in a relatively short period of time.

A permanent majority has to be earned. That starts with good policy. But it continues into other areas, as well.

Democrats will also have to avoid the kind of corruption and scandal that so often arises when parties hold majorities for too long. Much of the 2006 Democratic campaign to take back the House and Senate focused on how incredibly corrupt the Republican Party had become. There was the Jack Abramoff scandal, in which a well-connected lobbyist funneled illegal donations to Republicans in exchange for votes. There were scandals involving straight bribery that took down Congressman Bob Ney and others. Tom DeLay, the House majority leader, had to resign his seat after being indicted. And in the run-up to the election, it was revealed that Mark Foley had been making sexual advances toward underage congressional pages. All in all, it was a pretty ugly list—so ugly, in fact, that few paid attention to the Democratic scandals that were also unfolding.

Democratic Representative William Jefferson of Louisiana, for example, had his congressional office raided by the FBI in connection with a bribery investigation. Like the script of a poorly written 1980s mob movie, the FBI found over $90,000—in Jefferson's freezer. Three years later, he was found guilty on eleven of sixteen counts and sentenced to thirteen years in prison. Oops.

Congress can be a corrupting place and often attracts those who are especially inclined to participate in inappropriate activity. The ego and ambition required to get elected to Congress means that those who make it there tend to have a sense of invincibility. It's what inspires a congressperson to take a little trip on a lobbyist's dime or to steer a federal contract toward a friend. And as a collective force, it can destroy a party.

The Democrats are certainly not immune to that kind of corruption. When they held the House and Senate for twenty-six consecutive years, there were more than two dozen scandals involving Democratic members of Congress. The Republican Party may have a horrible track record on scandals, but to date, Democrats haven't done all that much better. And no one should expect the Democratic leadership to devise some magical plan that will prevent an individual member from participating in illegal and embarrassing activity.

But while some scandal is inevitable, the way the party leadership responds is not. There are really two significant ways that the Democratic Party can mitigate the damage that scandals can cause. The first is the "throwing under the bus" technique.

Unless the alleged scandal is so egregiously inaccurate that a full-throated defense would be required for the sake of justice and fairness, the party should refrain from protecting its accused members. All members of the Democratic caucus should understand that if they put themselves in a position in which they are acting criminally or unethically or if they are so reckless as to appear to be acting that way, they alone must be responsible for the consequences. In a court of law, innocence has to be presumed. But party politics cannot be played the same way—the burden of proof must be on the accused.

Part of why the Mark Foley sex scandal resonated so punishingly for the GOP was that it became clear that party leaders knew that Foley was acting inappropriately toward minors, but they sought to protect him rather than the victims. Had the Republicans thrown Foley under the bus earlier, they might have saved a few House seats. Instead, they protected an attempted child molester while campaigning for family values. Even birthers can appreciate that kind of irony.

The second thing the party needs to do when dealing with a scandal is to confront it harshly. Major figures should call on the corrupted member to resign. Privately, leaders should push for the same. Expulsion from Congress should always be on the table. If the Democratic Party takes the lead on this, it will be seen as strongly anti-corruption, even if Democrats are creating the scandals. That's the key. There is nothing that Barack Obama or Nancy Pelosi or Harry Reid or any other Democratic leader can do to prevent a politician from doing something exceptionally stupid. But when it happens, they can respond with fury and sharp retribution. If the leadership can make the scandal about the person and not the party, it's unlikely that the individual corruption will derail the permanent majority.

If the party is able to avoid the pitfalls of corruption and scandal, and if it can manage its internal divisions, it will be in pretty good shape, though still not out of the woods. Among other things, Democrats will have to deal with the risks that accompany an inevitable enthusiasm gap.

One of the most substantial long-term challenges for the party is to keep its base enthused, excited, and, most important, engaged. During the 2008 campaign, the gap in excitement between Democrats and Republicans was palpable. Obama's rallies were regularly attended by crowds of tens of thousands, all of whom were cheering with excitement and hoping desperately for change. In contrast, McCain often held rallies with fewer than 1,000 voters, sometimes at venues that remained more than half empty. Partly this was a function of Obama himself. His way of speaking and his historic candidacy combined to make the journey to the event worthwhile. But there was more to it than that. The Democrats had been out of the White House for eight years, during which time George W. Bush had effectively destroyed America's economy and global stature. His success in pushing a far-right agenda, his self-induced quagmire in Iraq, and his incompetent response to Hurricane Katrina—every last bit of it made Democrats crave a new direction. Obama was the perfect candidate for the moment, but it was the moment, as much as it was his candidacy, that took him to the White House.

In that kind of atmosphere, Democratic enthusiasm fueled hundreds of millions of dollars in small donations and millions of volunteers. Being out of power and feeling powerless combined to form the driving force that awakened the Democratic Party.

Fast forward a dozen years.

If the Democrats make it that long in the majority, the enthusiasm gap will become a legitimate problem. Members of the far right will have spent twelve years fuming as their vision of the country is obscured and obliterated. The desire for change among them will be rabid. Contrast that with the Democratic base, which will have, by then, enjoyed more than a decade in power as well as the tangible results that come with it.

Granted, the increasingly enthused Republican base will still hold vastly different viewpoints than most of the country, and the candidates it nominates will still face substantial obstacles upon nomination. But the excitement itself will weigh on the debate and, in some circumstances, change the narrative. During the health care debate, for example, throngs of overaggressive anti-reform protesters filled town hall meetings, disrupting conversation, but also transforming the way the media portrayed the story. The health care debate was defined as they, not the White House, intended. If the enthusiasm gap continues to widen, at some point, it may jeopardize the Democrats' ability to govern.

There are two ways that the Democratic Party can best confront the enthusiasm gap problem. The first is to put a premium on recruiting charismatic, politically skilled candidates. Too often, uninspiring, uninspired candidates try to ignite the Democratic base with awkward adherence to stilted talking points. Their speeches are dull at best and painful at worst. The more the population of Democratic politicians can be made up of engaging candidates, of people who actually have the ability to connect to voters, the better off the party will be.

Party leaders must also be careful to accurately manage the expectations of their voters. In his first year in office, Barack Obama engendered some disappointment among many of his core followers, in part because their expectations had been somewhat mismanaged during the campaign. Though he explicitly cautioned otherwise, many of Obama's most ardent supporters were disappointed with the speed at which Obama could actually deliver change. That kind of disappointment only widens the enthusiasm gap and makes the challenge of mobilizing the base more difficult.

Over time, the Democratic leadership and the White House need to work to ensure that they clearly define what they can accomplish in a period of time and then actually go out and get it done. Building that kind of trust between party and base is critical; in the end, it may be the difference between securing a permanent majority and watching it sail right by.

The next twenty-five years are a substantial piece of American history yet to be written. In that time, the success of the Democratic Party will be bolstered by changing demographics, a state-of-the-art organizational infrastructure, and an opposition party that is collapsing. But through that time period, the party's success will also depend on how it reacts to events it cannot (or does not) foresee.

As the Republicans learned in 2006 and in 2008, crisis and conflict can reorient the public's priorities. In 2002, Republicans gained seats in Congress *because* of the Iraq war. By 2006, public opinion had shifted so sharply against the war—and the president—that it catalyzed a Democratic takeover of Congress. Two years later, Republicans faced another painful reality, as the economic crisis erupted so dramatically that it became far and away the most important concern for the American voting population.

That same kind of public movement is bound to happen in the future. If a terrorist attack occurs on American soil, for example, national security might quickly replace the economy as the issue that Americans care most about. When the consequences of global climate change start surfacing in dramatic ways—when the Maldives are under water and Florida appears to be next—a new energy out-look will find its way quickly to the front of voters' minds.

How a Democratic president responds to the unfore-seeable will largely dictate whether the party remains in power. If national security becomes the country's top con-cern, how Democrats respond to national security situa-tions will be the only thing that really matters to voters. Were Democrats cautious and measured, but clear and forceful? Did they exercise leadership in a way that helped make the American people feel safer? Did they take ap-propriate action swiftly? Were they too timid? Too ag-gressive? Too intellectual? Too tone deaf?

Whatever their response, the dynamic will have changed, and the party will have to change with it. It was largely the Bush administration's response to September 11 that was its undoing. With carte blanche to do whatever they chose, senior Bush officials made some of the worst possible decisions for reasons that had little, if anything, to do with the national interest. A similarly situated Demo-cratic president, making equally reckless calls, could launch his or her party straight back to the minority.

The Democratic Party has never had a better opportu-nity to build a permanent majority. But not everything has fallen conveniently into place. Keeping hold of power for an entire generation will require a lot from a party that has, at times, failed to deliver. It will require that Democrats put a premium on finding compromise within their own ranks so that the conservative or progressive wings of the party don't single-handedly kill legislation. It will require the party to resist the temptation of bipartisanship, even though that word will continue to carry positive political buzz with it. When scandals arise, it will require a Democratic leadership that swiftly punishes those who committed wrongdoing and highlights its intolerance for political corruption.

More than anything, securing a permanent majority will require the Democratic Party to produce smart legislation, to react intelligently to crises and unforeseeable events, and to ensure that its message is aligned with that of the burgeoning progressive majority. It will require them to govern well. Democrats don't have to be perfect, but they need to prove that they're capable. If they can—if they're able to manage those hurdles and pitfalls—they'll be well on their way to governing the country for a generation to come.

TEN

☆ ☆ ☆

Getting It Right

It will be fun to see how the story ends.
—*Barack Obama, on Election Day 2008*

A lot can be said about the possible future achievements of the Democratic Party, but in that conversation, we shouldn't forget that Democrats haven't always exactly been a party to be proud of.

Take Andrew Jackson, for example. Old Hickory himself. Jackson was a famous war hero turned president who is best remembered for expanding democracy, staring down southern secessionists, reducing the national debt, and opposing a national bank. But Jackson was also a pretty big fan of ethnic cleansing. That's right—Andrew Jackson was responsible for the deaths of thousands of Native Americans. During his presidency, 45,000 Native

Americans were marched from their homes and forced to relocate. The Trail of Tears? That was his thing.

Then there was James K. Polk, who wanted to take California from Mexico—and did so by lining up troops on the Mexican border and picking a fight. And, of course, you can't forget Franklin Pierce and James Buchanan, both Democrats, both of whom defended the expansion of slavery while president. Which reminds me—I almost forgot to mention—the Democratic Party was also the party of slavery.

"I hold that in the present state of civilization," barked South Carolina Democratic Senator John C. Calhoun in 1837, "where two races of different origin, and distinguished by color, and other physical differences, as well as intellectual, are brought together, the relation now existing in the slaveholding States between the two, is, instead of an evil, a good—a positive good." Yep—a Democrat said that.

In Lincoln's famous second inaugural address, he describes the approaching Civil War this way: "Both parties deprecated war, but one of them would make war rather than let the nation survive, and the other would accept war rather than let it perish." The party that wanted to make war? You guessed it: the Democrats.

The twentieth century was a bit rocky, too. Woodrow Wilson, the first Democratic president of that century, took the United States into World War I and signed Espionage and Sedition Acts to suppress anti-war opinion while it was happening. War was actually a pretty popular trend for the emerging Democratic Party. Harry Truman sent troops to the Korean peninsula (where they remain to this day), and, of course, there was Vietnam, which was started by one Democrat and escalated by another. According to Robert Dallek's biography of Lyndon Johnson, *Flawed Giant,* the former president was once pressed by reporters at a private meeting to justify the American presence in Vietnam. Johnson lost his temper, unzipped his pants, and actually exposed himself to the group.

"This is why!" he shouted.

That, I'm afraid, is a true story about a Democrat.

Yes, there are many chapters in the history of the Democratic Party that are undeniably cringe-worthy and deeply, deeply regrettable. Jimmy Carter, for example. But, over time, the Democratic Party has evolved. The modern party, born out of the New Deal—out of the idea that government can be a tool for good—reshaped the direction of the country. Social Security and Medicare were Democratic ideas rooted in that philosophy. So were Head Start and Medicaid.

It was a Democratic president who helped rebuild Europe after World War II and a Democratic president who won the war in the first place. Democrats evolved over time in dramatic ways. The party that had championed Jim Crow laws in the South, that once counted Strom Thurmond and George Wallace as members, became the party of civil rights. A Democratic Congress passed the

Civil Rights Act and the Voting Rights Act and a Democratic president signed them into law. Discrimination based on race, gender, national origin, and age were all outlawed by Democrats. Democrats were responsible for the Family and Medical Leave Act, for labor unions, for both G.I. bills.

For decade upon decade, in the face of unrelenting opposition, it was Democrats who pushed for universal health care; in 2010, it was Democrats who delivered. And when climate change emerged as a central threat, Democrats, as always, took the lead.

Our greatest leaps forward, some of the most substantial progress we've ever made in this country, are rooted in the accomplishments and aspirations of Democrats.

Contrast that with the Republican Party, which started with the noblest of purposes and has since steadily devolved. Republicans used to be the party of Lincoln, founded on the principle of preventing the expansion of slavery. His presidency will always be a pretty big trophy for the GOP. There was also Ulysses S. Grant, who may have been fairly corrupt and often drunk, but he did win the Civil War for the Union, and he wrote a pretty great memoir.

There was Teddy Roosevelt, too, the father of natural conservation, the man most responsible for the existence of today's national parks, a progressive in the truest sense. But by the 1920s, the Republican Party came to represent an economic philosophy designed to benefit only the wealthy and the kind of political corruption that would define twentieth-century American politics. There was Warren Harding, whose bumbling nature and propensity for corruption were compounded by his insistence on writing his own speeches. Of his first inaugural address, H. L. Mencken wrote, "He writes the worst English that I have ever encountered. It reminds me of a string of wet sponges; it reminds me of tattered washing on the line; it reminds me of stale bean soup, of college yells, of dogs barking idiotically through endless nights."

He continued, "It is so bad that a sort of grandeur creeps into it. It drags itself out of the dark abysm of pish, and crawls insanely up the topmost pinnacle of posh. It is rumble and bumble. It is flap and doodle. It is balder and dash."

Still, that inauguration speech was probably the high point of presidential life for Harding, who spent his short time in office marred by scandals. The friends he appointed to cabinet positions collected bribes and stole from the government—often.

Harding's death meant Calvin Coolidge, another Republican, would become president long enough to extend the newfound tradition of bringing shame to the Republican Party. Coolidge would sleep between ten and twelve hours each day, venturing to be, as historian Marcus Cunliffe described, "the least president" the United States ever had. Coolidge probably caused the Great Depression, but it was Herbert Hoover, another Republican, who was there for the October 1929 crash. His economic program made things so much worse that it paved the way for Democrats to take control of the White House for twenty years.

Where Democrats reformed themselves for the better, the Republicans weren't quite as lucky. Years later, there was, of course, Richard Nixon, and with him Watergate. There was Gerald Ford, and with him the pardon of Nixon. There was Iran-Contra, steep cuts to social programs, opposition to civil rights, and tax cuts for the wealthiest few. Then there was George W. Bush, whose list of scandals, wars, breaches of duty, and violations of the Constitution so dwarfs those of his predecessors that he has come to define the GOP's point of no return. The Republican Party has come unraveled. An idea birthed by Lincoln himself, an organization once powered by a reasoned conservatism, the party has now shriveled into a regional club of the angry and ignorant, those who are sure the president is a socialist even if they aren't sure what socialism is.

In the weeks leading up to the 2008 election, documentary filmmaker Alexandra Pelosi (daughter of the Speaker of the House) interviewed several McCain/Palin supporters at political rallies, painting a vivid picture of what the Republican Party has become.

"What do McCain voters have in common?" Pelosi asked a Republican woman she pulled aside from the crowd. The woman knew the answer instinctively and answered without hesitating.

"We all hate the same things."

Those six words and that kind of worldview provide ample evidence of why a Democratic permanent majority is such a good idea. It's not just that Democrats are right on policy—though they are. It's not just that they would do a better job governing—though they would. It's not just that they are the party of fairness and justice and opportunity. It's that there are simply no circumstances under which Democrats would ever court those kinds of voters.

At Republican congressman Wally Herger's town hall meeting in late August 2009, a man stood up in the audience and declared himself a right-wing terrorist. The congressman responded, not by informing the police, but by telling the man he was a "great American." That's what the Republican Party has become. It is no longer a credible alternative.

That kind of narrow, venomous outlook, that kind of anti-intellectual, wholly irrational philosophy cannot be allowed back in control of the U.S. government. Any party that thinks government operates best when it is small, weak, and ineffective should not be in charge of operating any government. Grover Norquist, a famous right-wing activist and former president of Americans for Tax Reform, was quoted in the *Nation* in October 2008 describing government this way: "My goal is to cut government in half in twenty-five years, to get it down to the size where we can drown it in the bathtub." A party with that kind of perspective cannot be put in charge of making government work. It is as dangerous as it is senseless.

Had McCain won the presidency, it's hard to know what the country would look like today. But here's what we do know. In his short time in office, Obama executed an order to end the war in Iraq, ended federal restrictions on stem cell research, and signed into law the Equal Pay Act. He signed a sweeping health reform bill, expanding coverage to more than 30 million Americans. He ended America's use of torture, while dramatically improving our image abroad. According to a 2009 Pew polling report, "an average of 71 percent of [international] respondents had at least some confidence in the U.S. president's handling of world affairs. In 2008, when Bush was in the White House, the figure in those same countries was only 17 percent." A 2009 global survey (the Anholt-GFK Roper Nation Brands Index) found that the United States had gone from the seventh most admired country in the world to the first. It's no wonder Obama won the Nobel Peace Prize just for getting elected.

The president also signed a sweeping anti-tobacco law, ended DEA raids on medical marijuana dispensaries, and passed a landmark public service bill. He invested $60 billion in renewable energy and instituted the toughest fuel economy standards in history.

Because of his work, the economy is growing again. The financial system is intact and faces much tougher regulations going forward. The vast majority of the taxpayer money that was used to bail out the banks will be paid back in time for the midterm elections. Because of the president and Democrats in Congress, our economic future is much brighter.

None of these accomplishments would have been possible had McCain been elected. Not one. Tremendous progress can be made with Democrats in control of the federal government. And unknowable crises would surely be the result of a Republican resurgence. Without a stimulus package, how much worse off would the economy be? With a continuation of Bush's foreign policy, how long before the military would have reached its breaking point? Imagine what a McCain presidency could have done to the country—and the world.

It won't always go perfectly. Compromises will have to be made and deals will have to be cut. Successes certainly won't preclude failures. There will be dips in the polls, times when leaders fail to meet the mark, and times of disappointment and anger. But for the most part, it can be a time of great and lasting progress—the far-off dream of progressive America come true.

There will no doubt be those who question the appropriateness of a permanent majority, arguing that a single party having singular control of the federal government for that long is, by definition, undemocratic—that without the existence of two vibrant, equally powerful political parties, the American people will be left without a real choice.

But make no mistake about it: Democrats will hold power for the next quarter century only if they get elected to do so. Nothing about Democratic majority control would change anything about our political system. If Democrats are able to hold power for that long, it will be because the people wanted it that way. Every two years, there will still be an election. Voters will have the opportunity to reject the Democratic Party if they so choose.

This isn't a permanent majority via coup. It is democracy at its very core—an entire generation of voters democratically rejecting the kind of backward vision that has come to define the Republican Party.

In May of 2009, *Washington Post* columnist Eugene Robinson wrote, "At this point, I'm almost ready to start rooting for the Republicans. . . . No, not really. There's no 'mercy rule' in politics. . . . The thing is, though, that input from an effective, constructive opposition party would be good at this pivotal moment in the nation's history. If only such a party could be found."

Perhaps one of the best arguments against a Democratic permanent majority is that, while it would be a democratically elected one, having a party without a serious competitor wouldn't best serve the interests of democracy. Put simply, not enough viewpoints means not enough democracy.

But the existence of a permanent majority in the United States would not preclude multiple viewpoints from influencing legislation. Not that having such an influence produces better laws. Compromising, deal making, and negotiating all mean watering down legislation in some way, rarely leaving it as effective as the original draft. The stimulus debate is a perfect example. Economists were telling the White House that for the stimulus to work most effectively, it would have to be at least $1 trillion. But to get key Republicans to sign onto the bill in the Senate, Obama had to settle for a bill that was less than $800 billion—just enough to ensure it couldn't work as well as hoped. That's how it almost always is—very few things ever function better because they've been watered down.

That said, one of the things the American people learned during that health care debate—certainly one of the things that the left learned—is that there are plenty of opposing viewpoints readily heard in the House and Senate. The Blue Dogs tell us that. Unlike when Republicans controlled the federal government, the Democrats don't have the entire party lockstep under a unified platform. The ongoing debates between Blue Dogs and progressives might as well be between two reasonable, opposing parties, with fiscal conservatives who are weary of bloated deficits on the one hand and advocates for social justice, whatever the cost, on the other.

Besides, the Democrats are only going to get this majority if they deserve it. That means governing competently—honestly. It means presenting a strong progressive agenda and systematically working to pass it. It means leading with reason and rationality, responding calmly, but decisively, to the inevitably unforeseen. We'll only get our permanent majority if the Democratic Party does its job right. That alone makes the aim to achieve it worthwhile.

The opportunity to secure this kind of majority has never been better. And the ball is in our court. Success will be achieved based on the actions and decisions of Democrats—from those who lead the party to the millions of its members.

The Democratic populace has to stay active and engaged. The success of the party is in large part dependent on having just as many Democrats volunteering, contributing, and turning out to vote as did in 2008. We must seek out new and special voices to carry the torch. The left will have to push hard, pressuring future congresses and administrations not to take the easier road of moderate compromise when a more progressive choice is possible.

But the base must stay committed as well, even when the party comes up short. Politics is an extraordinarily complex chess game, and one that, no matter their advantages, Democrats will not always win. But over time, the effect of a long-term Democratic majority will mean the adoption of a progressive agenda that could achieve the kinds of lofty goals first envisioned in the philosophy of the New Deal, now adapted for the twenty-first century.

For their part, Democratic politicians must work hard to keep the trust of those who will drive their success. They need to continue to embrace minority communities and to solidify those realignments. More than anything, over the years, Democrats must produce. They should take their lessons from Ted Kennedy. Fight for the most progressive deal possible, but, in the end, take the best deal available. If the Democrats can keep producing progressive legislation, however imperfect, they can fix mistakes later. In the meantime, they can prove to the people who elected them that they are competent and, unlike the GOP, that they are actually capable of governing.

We are at the beginning of a new political era, and with it, a new obligation. This turning point in history has placed Democrats in a unique position. As a party, as a movement, we have, for the first time in decades, the chance to remake the country with an unapologetically progressive vision. Now is the time, more so than ever before, for the millions of Americans who call themselves Democrats and for the thousands who are elected to state and federal office to take up that challenge, to see that majority through to its permanency. The possibility of a generation of Democratic rule has finally emerged.

This is our chance to see it through.

ACKNOWLEDGMENTS

As with any work of this nature, the process of turning *Permanently Blue* from an idea into these two hundred pages was very much a collaborative process. I want to begin by thanking the team at the *Huffington Post*, especially Nico Pitney and Colin Sterling. In early 2008, I was given the opportunity to contribute regularly to the *Huffington Post*, where I developed some of the concepts that would ultimately find their way into this book. *Permanently Blue* grew out of a piece published there called "How Democrats Might Actually Build a Permanent Majority." Were it not for Nico and Colin, I would not have had a platform from which to begin making these arguments. My most sincere thanks to you both.

I am also grateful to my agent, Peter McGuigan, and the whole team at Foundry Literary Media. Peter's advice and suggestions helped shape the early proposal, and his unrelenting talents ensured that it found the right outlet. Peter, thank you for your guidance, your support, and your trust.

I am especially appreciative to Nathan Roberson, my editor at Three Rivers Press. Nathan may just be the most insightful person I've ever met. Each and every suggestion he made improved the quality of the manuscript. He is incredibly sharp, thorough, attentive, and is a brilliant writer in his own right. I count myself lucky to have had the chance to work so closely with him throughout this process.

Thank you also to the entire team at the Crown Publishing Group, especially to Rachel Klayman, who contacted me in 2008 and first gave me the confidence that the ideas I was expressing in op-eds could be expanded into book form. Without Rachel, this project never would have come to fruition.

Thank you to all of those who weighed in on the manuscript and offered their comments, advice, and revisions. A special thanks to my research assistants, especially Robert Lamontagne, whose efforts are evident on nearly every page.

To my parents, and Alana and Jordan—thank you for your abiding love and support throughout this entire process, and through all the years that led up to it. To my dad, in particular: thank you for letting me bounce just about every idea that ended up in the book off of you. Thank you for reading each chapter, through each iteration. You were the most important adviser of all.

Finally, and most important, thank you to my beautiful fiancée, Megan. If it wasn't for your editing skills, each chapter might have ended up as one giant run-on sentence. And if it wasn't for your love and your ability to share the joy of the process with me, this book would have ended up an unfinished manuscript. I love you. This book is dedicated to you.

INDEX

ABOUT THE AUTHOR

Dylan Loewe is a Democratic speechwriter and strategist and is a veteran of nearly two dozen campaigns. He is a regular contributor to the *Huffington Post* where he provides commentary and political analysis. He has written speeches and op-eds for politicians and public officials at the highest levels of government, CEOs of Fortune 500 companies, and leaders of some of the country's most influential nonprofit organizations.

Loewe holds a J.D. from Columbia Law School and a master's in public policy from the Kennedy School of Government at Harvard University. He also earned a B.A. in political science from UCLA, where he graduated magna cum laude and Phi Beta Kappa.